Defuse Your Pension Time-Bomb

How To Create A Generous Income Through Property Investment

By

John Doherty

Publisher: Whitestone Press, 10 Dragons Court, Crofts End Road, Bristol BS5 7XX.

ISBN 9781478305569

A CIP catalogue record for this book is available from the British Library.

Produced for Whitestone Press by Createspace

Disclaimer

The information in this book is set out in good faith for educational purposes only. The contents do not in any way constitute financial advice. You should seek independent professional advice before making any investment. No liability can be accepted for losses or expenses incurred as a result of relying on statements made in this book. Laws and regulations are complex and liable to change and readers should check the current position with the relevant authorities before making personal arrangements. Taxation information and legislation rules quoted are all correct as at 2012.

Investing in property can be a risky business just like any other investment. Historical growth in property prices does not necessarily mean that prices will increase in the future. Your property may be repossessed if you do not keep up the payments on your mortgage.

Editor: Peggy Ireland, BA, B Com.

Proofreaders: Annette Young. Deena Naish. (Avon Valley Secretarial Services. Email:avsecretarialdn@blueyonder.co.uk)

Cover design: Steven Peterson

Portrait Photo: Richard Tippett LBPPA www.digitaldreamsuk.co.uk

Dedication

To Ruth

Acknowledgements

I would like to thank my editorial team for their support and suggestions: David Bussy, Jerome Caballero, Robin Campbell, Ian Clark, Andrew Forbes, Donna Gaywood, Andrew Greenaway, David Hedley, Dave Hunt, Malcolm Mclean, Pat Moore, Deena Naish, Paul Scoplin and Louis Sherman. Thanks to Mandy for typing part of the manuscript. Thanks to all who agreed to share their story in the case studies. Thanks to Kevin Green for the foreword. Thank you to all my teachers.

Table of Contents

Case Studies

Foreword

It's an easy trap to fall into. We all lead busy lives and many people overlook planning for their retirement. Too many people fall victim to the major pension and investment companies, who often take large fees and commissions. Pensions have halved in their performance values in recent years and pay-outs on drawdown are not as predicted at the outset.

John Doherty has a refreshing outlook on using the alternative of property investment as a more robust tool to provide for a secure retirement. As a multi-millionaire businessman, I like being in control of my own assets, rather than have a middle-man do the job for me; and take some of my profits at the same time! The pension companies often invest your money in the asset class of property as it's seen as a safe option. John encourages us to cut out the middle-man and drive our own futures and fortunes. As one of the UK's largest private sector property landlords, I am an example of someone who (despite being homeless in 1984) is now extremely financially secure through property investment. I can recommend this book as an easy read and a great starting point to the property investment business.

I have helped hundreds of people achieve financial freedom through property investment and other business strategies. You can find out more at http://www.kevingreen.co.uk and attend one of our cost-effective wealth training sessions. As John states in this book, learn your business well before you take the first step. The dedication, persistence and hard work that you put into your wealth building now, if executed properly, will look after you financially for life. It can also be a huge asset to those who will benefit from your inheritance.

Well done, John, and a very thoughtful, insightful, entertaining, clear and inspiring book.

Kevin Green is a self-made multi-millionaire and social entrepreneur. He is one of the UK's largest residential property landlords and a multi-business owner. The 48-year-old dyslexic, who featured on Channel 4's Secret Millionaire and Channel 5's Secret Interview, was homeless in 1984. Today, his property portfolio runs into the hundreds. He has a wealth of experience in the property investment world and heads a number of successful companies and other non-property related businesses. He is also involved in coaching under his own brand of Kevin Green Wealth (KGW) and is a 'Dynamo' role model for the Welsh Government, inspiring young people in schools and universities to set up businesses. He has helped launch the new Entrepreneurship Academy Wales for the business leaders of the future.

Before making his fortune in business, he was a successful dairy farmer. In 1999 he won a Nuffield Scholarship in agriculture and studied the attitudes and personalities of high achievers. He interviewed Bill Gates and Sir Richard Branson. The wealth guru loves to educate, motivate and inspire others; and his passion and enthusiasm are quite infectious. His down-to-earth approach is often referred to by those who know him as being 'exactly what it says on the tin'. These qualities have catapulted him into worldwide demand as a speaker at conferences, dinners and seminars.

Introduction

The principles outlined in this book are not just the result of five years of training and experience in property investing. They are time-proven concepts, which you can apply with confidence. There are already many well-written books on the subject of property investment in the UK. I have not sought to rewrite these, so this book does not claim to be a complete guide to buy-to-let.

Most books, however, are written with the assumption that you are already convinced of the benefits of property investment. I do not make that assumption. Consequently I have given more space to setting out the numerous possibilities offered by property. I have also taken the time to consider many of the common objections.

Property investing has been hailed as a sure route to wealth. But it may also be regarded simply as an alternative route to a comfortable retirement. My research into the pension crisis has revealed the failures of the traditional pension. While contacting several pension experts and journalists via Twitter and email, I received a reply which gave the project more urgency. Malcolm Mclean, senior pensions consultant at Barnett Waddingham and writer for the Daily Mail wrote:

"Good luck and best wishes with the production of your book. The more people that are encouraged to make financial provision for their old age themselves by whatever means, the better it will be for them and for society at large. At the risk of sounding too apocalyptic, I believe that one of the biggest social and economic challenges we face in this country is how to cope with the problems of a rapidly ageing population – both now and even more so in the future as the ratio of workers to pensioners continues to fall and the prospects for those under-pensioned and under provided for becomes ever more grim."

I have provided some tools to help you work out your own personal pension deficit.

We live in the digital age. So the debate does not have to end with the last chapter of this book. The website is designed as a resource, with lots of information to help you build a healthy property portfolio. You can also get in touch. It would be great to hear about your experiences.

I hope you will find this book helpful. May you enjoy reading it as much as I have enjoyed writing it.

About the Author

Returning to the UK in 2002 after a number of years abroad, John and Ruth Doherty had nothing. They couldn't even get a council house for their small family. If not for their kind-hearted sister-in-law who took them into her home, they wouldn't have had a roof over their heads.

In less than a week John found work in his trade as an electrician. He saved up and with the help of family was eventually able to buy his first house. Still he struggled, stretching his pay from week to week, so in 2004 he decided to start his own electrical business.

One day in 2006, John bought a book from the business section of WH Smith called *Rich Dad, Poor Dad*. He thought it was about teaching children to handle money. This book was a revelation. It introduced him to the concepts of property investing and passive income. He decided to do more research on the subject. He was fortunate to have a customer who had a substantial portfolio, and who explained how he had accomplished his goals.

The couple bought their first buy-to-let property in June 2007. Since then they have continued to learn and to invest. Their portfolio of properties is valued to date at more than £800,000. They have faced the challenges of investing in property in the midst of a recession. Today there is enough equity in the portfolio to make them mortgage-free with cash to spare.

In 2010 John started Whitestone Property Services; providing reliable, reasonably priced, building services to his customers.

He also runs a one-on-one consultancy service for people who want to get started in property investment.

John's loves are travel, nature photography, scuba diving, and his family.

Chapter One

Your retirement – comfort or crisis?

How would you like to spend your retirement?

Have you ever taken the time to think about retirement? Midlife can be a very busy time. The main focus is often on raising a family, paying your mortgage and enjoying life as much as possible. When, like me, you pass the half-century milestone, you begin to see your silver years approaching fast on the horizon.

We all know deep down that we need to do something about our pension. This book is written to help you do just that. So now you've taken one step in the right direction, you can feel better. In this short guide we'll confront the uncomfortable reality which is up ahead for future UK pensioners. Then we'll show you how to harness the power of the property market to your advantage.

The savings of the majority

are woefully insufficient.

The idyllic vision versus the stark reality

How do you envisage your ideal retirement? Most TV adverts aimed at the older generation portray a life of ease and comfort. There's usually a picture of a greying couple seated on a deck chair near the beach. A Caribbean cruise or a holiday home in France may be suggested. Your own aspirations may be quite simply to enjoy more leisure, spending time in the garden and treating your grandchildren from time to time. It was not so long ago that people anticipated retiring earlier and enjoying life while they could still walk without the aid of a Zimmer frame.

But times have changed. By now everyone in Britain should be aware that UK pensions are in trouble. Governments and financial institutions have known for some time that the savings of the majority of people in the UK are woefully insufficient to fund a financially secure retirement. Instead, many can anticipate what Martin Lewis of MoneySavingExpert.com has termed the *Cold Baked Bean Retirement*.

Research by pension provider LV has shown that the average retired couple in the UK spends £17,922 a year for living expenses. Rising utility bills and food prices, low interest rates and inflation have combined to dramatically increase the cost of living over the past five years. As a result, more than 6 million people over the age of fifty are planning to work beyond retirement age to make ends meet. Age UK says that more than 3 million pensioners are in fuel poverty, forcing them to choose between eating and heating.

What does retirement mean to you?

Perhaps the idea of retirement is not one that fills you with joy. If you love your job, and there are many who do, you may prefer to keep working. Maintaining your network of colleagues and friends can have its advantages. In this book I will take a look at the traditional idea of retirement and show that retiring is not just about stopping work. It's about having the freedom to choose.

Life expectancy in the UK has been increasing since the end of World War II. A man who retires at sixty-five can now look forward, on average, to thirteen years of leisure. Early retirement and a longer than average life could easily increase this to over thirty years. It's almost another lifetime! What many people fail to recognise is that their wants and needs will change dramatically over these years.

I was asked by a stonemason to do some electrical work on his new retirement property. He was moving to Portishead, a small town on the banks of the Severn Estuary. In my mind, I conjured up a vision of a cottage overlooking the sea. I was surprised to find that he had bought a three-storey house with long sets of steps going down from the street to the front door, down again to the basement garage/workshop and up to the first floor. It was the workshop that swung it for him. His idea of retirement was to potter around, fixing things and making things. Those steps, however, were not going to be very practical for his old age and that of his wife.

When planning for retirement, we need to understand that there will be a period of leisure and activity, followed by a season of physical decline. In the first part you will need funds to enjoy yourself. In later years funds may be channelled into paying for care.

The growing pension crisis

This generation may be the first since World War II who cannot expect a better standard of living than the previous generation. News reports remind us almost daily that there is a major crisis in the funding of pensions. While researching the pension crisis, I found out that the pension time bomb is due to explode in exactly the same year that I should have been retiring – 2027!

In chapter two we'll take a closer look at the scale of this pension crisis. We will seek to discover why things are getting worse for the baby-boomer generation.

Pensions are a complex subject and it can be baffling for most people to work out exactly what they can expect to receive. I will attempt to explain the various pension schemes and help you to work out how much you can expect to get. Then I will show you how to calculate your projected expenses when you are no longer working. In this way you will be able to make an approximation of your own pension deficit.

The pension time bomb is due

to explode in 2027.

We'll take a closer look at the efficiency of traditional pensions in providing a secure financial future. We will identify the factors, such as charges and inflation, which erode the value of our pensions. And we'll challenge the assumption that the state will take care of us in old age.

Why property?

In chapter three, we'll introduce the concept of investing in property for a more comfortable retirement. Those who know, use property as a time-proven method for building wealth. We will examine the numerous options that property can give us.

The average age of first-time home buyers has been rising in recent years. According to some estimates it is now about forty. We'll also look at how younger buyers can get onto the property ladder much earlier.

I love the water. I once canoed down the Ardèche Gorge in France – a six-hour journey. We had the flow of the river to help us along, but even so, we had to do a fair bit of rowing. Rowing is a bit like saving for your pension. It can be hard work. Another sport I would like to try is sailing. The closest I've got so far is wind surfing. The power of the wind propelling me along was exhilarating, when I wasn't falling into the water! When you invest in property, you have the power of the market behind you. In chapter four I will show you four ways to harness the potential of the property market.

Harness the potential
of the property market.

Dealing with misconceptions and fears

Maybe you've already considered investing in property. But you've been put off by reports in the media. You need to remember that headlines are written with one eye on newspaper sales. Unfortunately it appears that bad news sells better than good news. Reports in the media can also be conflicting. One day there will be an article reporting a crash in house prices. The next day another paper will run a story on house price rises. For this reason newspapers are not usually the best source of accurate information for the property investor.

It is important to know who to listen to when taking advice. The friend you meet down at the pub may warn you that property investment is risky. Has he tried it? What qualifies him to give advice? When you read an article announcing that house prices will fall, check who wrote it. If it's by someone linked to a stock market investment company, then you'll know their agenda. To get the right advice you need to look in the right place. In chapter five we'll try to debunk some common misconceptions. A popular objection is that it takes money to make money. "If I had some money I would definitely invest in property, but at the moment I am just struggling to make ends meet." However, we'll see that you may be sitting on a pile of money which is more than enough to get you started. I will show you how to unlock the capital tied up in your home to use as a deposit for a buy-to-let investment.

The overriding factor holding most people back is fear. What if the market crashes? What if I lose my house? What if the sky falls on me? Fear has stopped more people succeeding than any other factor. It is true that property investing, like all forms of investing, is not without risks. Some of the horror stories are true. We've heard of people who have overstretched themselves and have lost a lot of money. A reasonable amount of caution is sensible. But blind fear can paralyse you and stop you realising your potential. We'll look at how fear grows in the absence of knowledge. We will see how learning can dramatically reduce the risks of failure. We will also identify the greatest risk of all; doing nothing.

Laying a foundation for a sound investment

Recently I was watching the news about an expedition to the North Pole. Why anyone would want to go there is beyond me, but it is generally considered to be a great achievement. Now if you woke up one day and said, "I'd like to go to the North Pole." what is the first thing you would do? Would you throw some clothes and a toothbrush in a bag and set off for the airport? Of course not. Preparation is crucial to success in all expeditions. Similarly, you need to make careful preparations in order to get the most out of property investment.

Today is a great time

to make a healthy profit.

This is particularly true in a slow market. Some of the people who appeared on Sarah Beeny's programme, *Property Ladder,* used to amaze me. They didn't listen to her advice, but ran off, following their own ideas. If I had an expert like Sarah Beeny helping me with property development I would be hanging on her every word. Yet despite the gaffes, the story usually had a happy ending. The developer made a profit because of one major factor: a fast rising market. In Sarah's later programme, *Property Snakes and Ladders,* things changed. The developers often ended up moving into their properties, as they were unable to sell them for a profit. The series was filmed just as the credit crunch was taking hold. It was shelved in 2009. You need to know what you are doing to succeed in today's market. But if you learn the ropes, today is also a great time to make a healthy profit.

Before you begin to invest in property it is important to take stock of your finances and to check out your credit report. Above all it is important to begin building a business mind-set. It is time to wake up to the reality that neither the government nor your employer is going to provide you with the retirement that you hope for. Alongside your job, you need to be nurturing a source of passive income. Money to add to your pension provision and to give you more options.

A growing number of people are taking property investment to a new level. Through case studies and testimonials we'll discover how some have become full-time landlords or property developers. It's not hard to fall in love with the property business and you might discover a passion that will fuel a new career.

Property investing

is a team sport.

Meet the professionals

Property investing is a team sport. It is important for you to know that you do not have to do everything by yourself. There are professionals whose services are essential to the purchasing process, such as mortgage brokers and solicitors. There is also a full range of services available to assist you in buy-to-let. This can be a bit of a maze to negotiate and you need to be aware that not all companies provide a reliable and cost effective service. I'll introduce you to some of the professional services whose experience you can use. I'll also give some pointers to help you evaluate them.

There are many ways to get into property. The route you choose will depend upon your objectives, your resources and your skill set. Everyone is different and what suits one person may not suit another. With property you have choices. If you're planning to take the DIY approach make sure you learn all you can first. I'll provide an introduction to some of the training which is available to help you. In this way you can benefit from the knowledge of others' mistakes and successes.

Your first investment property

Chapter eight will take you through the process of finding, buying and letting a house. Even if you decide to employ the services of a property professional, it is important for you to know how things work. It is beyond the scope of this book to explore all the details. However, by helping you to grasp the basics, you can go on from there. In the section on further reading and on the website I list some of the available literature.

So you are a landlord. What next?

In chapter nine we'll look at the two major difficulties faced by investors, tenant problems and running out of money. Buy-to-let can become buy-to-fret if you are ill-prepared and slow to react. We'll see how to reduce the risk of potential problems.

A lot of effort usually goes into building your property portfolio. So much so, that it is easy to overlook the long-term view. To achieve your investment's maximum potential, and to avoid giving too much to the taxman, it's important to do some long term planning. I will give you some pointers on tax planning and exit strategies.

Chapter ten will outline some of the other ways to invest in property. SIPPs are now a preferred option for pension savings. They can now be used as a tax-free way to accumulate a property pension. Property investment can be more diverse than the traditional buy-to-let model. We'll show you other ways of using letting to produce extra income and to save for retirement.

A call to action

This book is a call to action. It's not about blaming the government or anyone else for the pension apocalypse our generation faces. Nor is it about wringing our hands and burying our head in the sand. We can't afford that luxury. We set out to help you put together an action plan; one that will give you the wealth you need to provide for your old age. Others around you and those who come after you can also benefit from your investments. This will only be possible if you take action. As they say: People who are always waiting for their ship to come in usually miss the boat!

Look up and see the opportunities that are available to you today. Many thousands of people in the UK and around the world are preparing for a brighter retirement by investing in property. Will you be one of them?

Chapter Two

The pension deficit: a ticking time bomb.

One of the greatest challenges facing the UK today is the pension deficit. In layman's terms this means that the National Insurance contributions of the current workforce are increasingly insufficient to fund the state retirement pension. Additionally, the majority of people don't have sufficient savings in private pensions. As a result, a growing number of pensioners are struggling to afford the kind of retirement they anticipated. Many today are even unable to cope with everyday expenses.

In this chapter we'll take a closer look at the question of pensions. If the subject is not one which inspires you, stay with me, because this will affect us all sooner or later. Finding out the truth now can give you a better chance of improving your pension prospects. In the 1974 film, *Towering Inferno*, when the architect was told about the fire he asked, "Just how bad is it?" I will ask the same question, but I'll also offer you a solution to help avoid disaster. First, a look at the various types of pension available today.

The UK state pension

On a cold January day in 1909, over 500,000 poor and elderly people queued to collect their first pension of five shillings (25p). The Old Age Pension was the first state-funded benefit of its kind. Up until the twentieth century, poverty had been viewed almost as a crime and the poor were often forced to pay their dues in a debtor's prison or a workhouse. Other acts of parliament followed that added to the state provision for pensioners. The legislation was designed to build a social security safety net for all UK residents. The National Insurance Act of 1946 completed the process by introducing free health care for all.

The state pension has been a mainstay of the social security system for many years. Many people have no other pension and in the past this has not mattered. It has been evident for some time, however, that a crisis is looming. Successive governments have tried but failed to address the problem of the pension deficit. It's now clear that the state pension alone will be insufficient for a comfortable retirement. The basic weekly pension stands at £102 in 2012, whereas average living costs are around £345 per week. Malcolm Mclean, a senior pensions consultant, sums up the situation, "The state pension will certainly be less than many might aspire to have in order to live comfortably in retirement."[i] Consequently, many pensioners today are forced to rely on means-tested benefits to help make up the shortfall.

Company pensions

In addition to the state pension, many workers pay into a company pension scheme. Most twentieth century employees could expect to have a job for life. Even unskilled labourers had a lifetime of guaranteed employment and a good pension afterwards. We live near to Cadbury's old chocolate factory near Bristol, South Gloucestershire. (It does look a bit like Charlie's chocolate factory). Many members of my wife's family have worked at the Somerdale plant at one time or another. Although it was often a monotonous job, Cadbury's employees enjoyed a good wage, many benefits and generous pension arrangements. It is not unknown for retired Cadbury's workers to be taking several holidays a year to exotic destinations.

But in 2010 the last Crunchy bar rolled off the production line at Somerdale. Production has now been moved to Poland. This kind of well-paid job-for-life with a generous pension is becoming increasingly rare. In the future people may have to start a new career up to four or five times in the course of their working life. Company pension schemes, if they exist, are often optional.

Work longer, pay more,

receive less.

There has also been a huge reduction in expected pension returns. Some estimate the annual income produced by a typical pension to be less than a third of the amount received by the last generation (see Annexe 2, Annuity Rates).

Pension experts are warning of a coming apocalypse. Mclean states in his article, *Mind the Generation Gap*, "As things stand at the moment, producing the level of pension income enjoyed by substantial numbers of former workers previously in the private sector will clearly be well beyond the reach of many in the years ahead."[ii]

Many companies used to offer a final salary pension scheme to long-term employees. Under this arrangement, the retired worker was guaranteed a percentage of his or her last salary as a pension. Very few of these schemes remain, as the companies cannot afford to fund the shortfall between the annuity income and the pension pay-outs.

Concern has also been expressed among providers that many people are accumulating several small pension pots with different companies, partly due to frequent redundancies. As a result of the confusion, there is an estimated £1 billion in unclaimed pension funds in the UK.

Public sector pensions

Civil servants, such as teachers, nurses and firemen, will receive a public pension in addition to their state pension. The government, as employer, pays into this, adding to the pension holder's own contributions. This used to be a generous pension and was one of the major benefits of working for the state. However the government has realised that some of these pensions are becoming unaffordable. As a result the goal posts are being moved. There have been many protests and strikes by public sector workers who are outraged at being told they will have to work for longer, may have to pay more, and may receive less from their pension.

How do pensions work?

The pension landscape has become very complex over the past number of years. So it isn't surprising that many people are in the dark about what they are entitled to. Do you know what date you are due to receive your state pension? (I thought I did, but I have just discovered it is now two years later!) Do you know how much you will receive and how it is calculated?

State pension: You pay into the state pension through your National Insurance contributions. When you reach official retirement age you will receive your pension. The amount is set by the government and is the same for everyone. As we have seen, this pension is not enough to fund your retirement even though it is increased every year.

Private pension: If you have a private pension you and your employer may both contribute. You also receive tax relief on your contribution. In effect the government tops up your pot by an extra 20% (or more if you are a higher rate taxpayer). Your pension provider (such as Standard Life, or Legal & General) then invests this money in the stock market or other investment vehicles. The fund manager's job is to grow your pension pot.

The age at which you can start to draw this pension is currently fifty-five. However, the longer you wait and the more you contribute, the greater the return, at least in theory. At retirement age you count up the total accumulated in your pension pot. You are allowed to draw out up to 25% of this sum tax free, if you choose. With what is left you are advised to shop around and buy an annuity. An annuity works a bit like a reverse insurance policy. You put down a lump sum and in return you receive an income for the rest of your life. Your monthly pension amount will depend on the size of the pension pot, your age at retirement, your health and a host of other factors (see Annexe 3 for typical returns in 2011).

Here is an example drawn from today's market: a contribution of £200 a month for twenty-five years means you will save £60,000. Add to this your tax breaks and the growth achieved by your fund and your final pension pot could be around £140,000. This sum could buy you an annuity to produce an annual income of around £8,400 per year. That's £700 per month or £161.54 per week.

Factors which force down pension returns.

So far, so good. But that isn't the whole story. Your money is being eroded by several factors.

Your money is being eroded.

Firstly, there are the charges. Every company applies a different charge rate to its pension products. In our illustration the pension pot ended up at £140,000. This is assuming your pension provider has a low rate of charges for its services. Using a high-charging company could reduce the size of your pot to around £103,000, giving a weekly pension of £119.23. That's £42 less each week – for life!

The Daily Mail pensions writer, Dan Hyde, has spoken of *opaque charges* on pension accounts. "Millions of pension investors are seeing their funds eaten away by charges that can leave them tens of thousands of pounds worse off in old age."[iii] He exposes the scandal of industry bosses who do not want people to know about high pension charges, claiming it might discourage them from saving.

Secondly, there is the confusion among pension holders as to how to get the most out of their pension pot. Some annuities have lower costs and give a better return than others. A recent report by the National Association of Pension Funds has revealed the lack of transparency and "dodgy dealing" of some annuity providers. They don't do enough to inform retirees to shop around for the lowest priced and best performing product.

This subject is complicated for most people, and the system is in great need of simplification. For years top executives in the finance industry have been helping themselves to large salaries and high bonuses, paid for by millions of savers. But just as Dorothy's dog Toto pulled the curtain back to reveal the mighty Wizard of Oz as an ordinary man, so the veil is now being lifted on the exclusive world of leading financial institutions.

Then there is inflation. The effect of inflation is to erode the value of cash with the passage of time. A payment of £161 may seem like a good amount today, but in relative terms, how much will it be worth in twenty-five years? Most annuities are arranged so that once your pension income is fixed it will not rise in line with inflation.

Other factors have eaten into the value of pension funds in recent years. Gordon Brown's decision in 1997 to stop tax credit reclaim (tax pensions), wiped billions of pounds off their value. The poor performance of the stock market in the years following the credit crunch of 2008 has set pension fund growth back enormously. The Bank of England's policy of quantitative easing has also had a huge negative impact on the value of pension funds.

I was working recently with a painter and decorator. He proudly announced that he was retiring at the end of the week. Then he explained that he had planned to retire five years earlier, but had decided to keep working due to the poor performance of his pension. Millions of people today are in a similar situation.

The ability of pensions to provide a secure financial future has been greatly reduced in recent times. The main reason is the poor performance of the stock market. Andrew Oxlade, editor of the Daily Mail's financial website, thisismoney.co.uk, says, "Millions of savers may be set for a shock from their next pension statement after the City regulator signalled that projections for returns will be dramatically slashed."[5]

Why are things so bad for this generation?

The proportion of retirees to working people is changing. The baby-boomer generation of children were born between 1945 and 1965. Population growth tailed off in the 60s partly due to contraception and partly due to materialism. The baby-boom bulge has been moving through the population graph like a tennis ball through a hosepipe. The first of the boomers reached sixty-five in 2010. There will be a steady increase in the number of senior citizens in the years leading up to 2030. Some experts, such as Tom McPhail, head of pension research at Hargreaves Lansdown, believe that fifteen years from now, the number of people alive over the age of eighty will have increased from 3 million to 4.7 million.[iv] Between now and 2030, the number of people eligible for state pension in the UK will increase continuously.

You may say, no problem, I paid my National Insurance all my life so the money is there to fund my pension. Not so. As we have seen, the money you paid in has now been spent on previous retirees and your pension must be paid for by the National Insurance contributions of current workers. As the workforce shrinks in proportion to the number of pensioners, the deficit is becoming more acute.

People are also living longer. Improved healthcare, the reduced number of smokers and a shift away from heavy manual work such as mining, are factors contributing to the improved life expectancy of people in the UK. The steady rise in life expectancy is set to continue. In 2012 men live, on average, until seventy-eight, and women until eighty-two. These figures were sixty and sixty-five respectively in 1940 according to one source. The government, in addition to raising the age at which you can draw the state pension, has proposed linking retirement age to life expectancy. State retirement age is gradually being increased to sixty-eight and may continue to rise.

What lies ahead?

Despite the frequent headlines about the pension crisis, many people today are still unprepared for retirement. Some are in denial; others are struggling just to make ends meet in the face of rising fuel, food and utility costs. Becky Barrow warns of a pending pension apocalypse. "Nearly half of the over-fifties will be forced to work until they are at least seventy-seven to enjoy a comfortable old age."[v] She quotes Joanne Segars, of the National Association of Pension Funds, who said, "Millions of workers are in for a rude wake-up call when they find they cannot afford to retire and instead see their retirement date slipping away into the distance. Those who do not want a fall in their living standards when they retire face a stark choice: work longer or save more, or do both."[vi]

Dan Hyde quotes pensions experts who predict that, "Babies born in 2012 will face sixty-year working careers because they will not get their state pension until they hit eighty."

UK pensioners in 2012

The situation for many UK pensioners is already pretty grim. "British pensioners are among Europe's poorest, with more than two million older people at risk of poverty," says Sarah Cassidy, of the Independent.[vii] Those with no supplementary pension have to rely on means-tested benefits such as pension credit and housing benefit. This wartime generation is not always comfortable accepting benefits. It was estimated that in 2011 over £3.5 million in pensioner benefits remained unclaimed. If all the help available was getting to those who need it, up to 700,000 pensioners could be taken out of poverty.

Millions of pensioners are being forced to cut back on their expenditure. Up to half a million have returned to work and over a quarter of a million are relying on financial assistance from their families. Their problems are compounded by the long term low interest rates. Those with savings are seeing very little return, leaving many to wonder why they bothered to save.

The Sweetie Jar test

I started paying into a private pension in 2002, saving £100 a month. Five years later I came home from work one day to find my annual pension statement had arrived in the post. Sitting down in the kitchen I opened it and checked how much I had in my pension pot. I saw the estimated monthly income this would produce. Not much. Then I looked at a sweetie tin on the worktop and decided to try a test. If I were to put all the money I had saved into a jar until I was sixty-five, then start spending it at the rate I had been quoted, what age would I be when it ran out? Quite old! This calculation was one of the factors that made me look into property investment.

The Sweetie Jar Test based on 7% annual growth:

Save £100 month for 25 years. Cost to you, £30,000. Pension pot, £84,100.

Annual income at 65, £4,870, or £93.65 per week.

Spend £93.65 per week from your sweetie jar and your £30,000 will last for 6 years and 2 months. You will be 71 before you start to get out more than you put in.

Try out the Sweetie Jar test next time you receive a pension forecast.

Is it worth paying into a pension?

It is good to pay into a pension scheme, especially if your employer is also contributing. A great advantage of a pension is the tax relief on your contributions. It's good to get something back from the taxman for once – a great feeling! Those who pay into a pension should ensure the charges are as low as possible. You should also seek to have some control over how the funds are invested. This is now possible though a SIPP (Self-Invested Personal Pension). However, not everyone will be able to ensure a comfortable retirement through a traditional pension. If you are self-employed, or if you have no company pension, then your contributions alone may not be enough, especially if you start late.

You need to ask yourself if there is not a more efficient way to create a pension nest egg.

Chapter Three

Why invest in property?

Who is investing in property today?

Property is the cornerstone of wealth creation. An examination of the Forbes rich list will reveal that a high proportion of millionaires made their money through property. Those who became wealthy through business often rely on property to protect their fortunes.

Lord Sugar is best known for his success with Amstrad and his TV series, *The Apprentice*. But where is his money now? It's in property. He buys and sells large hotels and makes a lot of money. He doesn't even like property, saying the only fun is when you buy and when you sell. But he cannot ignore its power in wealth creation.

Property is the cornerstone of wealth creation.

Queen Elizabeth II has a significant portion of her fortune in property. Aside from the state-owned castles and palaces, she owns a lot of commercial and residential property.

Many members of the cabinet have money invested in property. The same is true for the shadow cabinet. Most politicians are aware of the importance of property as a means to create and protect wealth.

Many Chinese business owners and other overseas millionaires are investing in property in the UK. London is considered the second best city in the world, after New York, for capital growth on property investment. In these uncertain times, property is a safe haven for those with money to invest.

If I asked you what the core business of McDonalds is, you would most likely say, selling hamburgers. But you would be wrong. McDonalds' main business is property. They are one of the world's largest owners of commercial property. Every restaurant is owned by them and leased to the franchisees. The sale of burgers is what allows their tenants to pay the rent and make a living.

Now you might be thinking that because the wealthy invest in property, then only they are able to do so. However, this is not the case. Property investment is rapidly becoming a major source of accumulated wealth for thousands of ordinary people in the UK today. Private rentals now make up 16% of the market in England.[viii] The sector has seen a large increase since 2003. Many hundreds of thousands of people, both professionals and manual workers, have discovered the power of property investment.

If you own your own home, you are also a property investor. The problem is you need to own more than one in order to profit from property.

What can property investment do for me?

At this point you may be expecting me to tell you that you can become a millionaire. Well many people have become millionaires through property investment, but maybe this isn't a priority for you. Let's stick instead to more down-to-earth, easily achievable goals. In this chapter I will outline some of the possibilities of property investment.

Provide an additional income

One benefit of sound property investment is cash flow. This means a regular income to supplement your salary. As employees, we are used to going to work and getting paid, spending our money, then going back to work to earn more. Although this is normal today, it was not always so. The Industrial Revolution brought multitudes of people from life on the farm to work in burgeoning mills and factories. Exchanging labour for an hourly rate was foreign to country people who were used to living from harvest to harvest. In the twenty-first century the first question we are asked on making a new acquaintance is often, "What do you do?" More than ever, we are defined by our job.

In our house we like to watch the BBC dramatizations of Jane Austen's novels. *Pride and Prejudice* portrays the growing romance between Elizabeth Bennett and Mr. Darcy. Did you ever wonder what Mr. Darcy and his friends did for a job? They were part of the "landed gentry". This meant they lived off the rents generated by the properties on their land. That is why they had so much time to gad about and drink tea with the ladies. For many years, only the wealthy could afford to invest in property. Now, thanks to more accessible finance brought in with the buy-to-let mortgage in the 1990s, an income from property is within the reach of a greater number of people.

Case study – Jim

The view from the top.

At an early age I saw the importance of owning your own home. My parents always rented and were constantly worried about the future. When my father retired he had nothing. We were married in 1970 and bought our first home. After losing money on a stock market investment, I started thinking about investing in bricks and mortar, which I could see and touch. Being an accountant, and a canny Scotsman, I did endless calculations taking into account interest rate variations and house price rises. I could see it made sense to invest in property.

We bought our first student house in 1985, using money from our own house as a deposit. This property is now worth fourteen times what we paid for it. The rental income for this coming year alone is more than the original purchase price in 1985. Since then we have continued investing and have built up a substantial portfolio.

The greatest difficulties I have encountered were in handling people. Some parents of my student tenants start with the assumption that the landlord must be a rogue and are quick to complain about every problem. I have learned to keep things in context. It is better to repair breakages quickly and keep the tenants happy, than to let things drag on. I am pleased to say I have had many cards thanking me for being a wonderful landlord.

Our most nail-biting time was following Black Wednesday in 1992, when interest rates soared to 15%. It was a period of severe financial difficulty for us and for everyone else at the time.

On the benefit side, I would have to say that our investment strategy has worked very well. We enjoy a comfortable retirement and are able to help others and treat our family. The low interest rates at the moment mean that our income from property is even higher than projected.

My top tip to investors starting out is, be cautious. Walk before you run. Buy one property and get settled. Then wait for a few years and buy another one. Steady does it.

Some investors have completely replaced their employment income with income from their property portfolio. In his book, *"Wage Slave to Financial Freedom"* Neil Mansell tells how he was able to say goodbye to the corporate world thanks to the generous passive income provided by his investments.

Retire when you choose, not when you are told you can

A good property investment can supplement or even replace a traditional pension. As we have seen in the previous chapter, UK pensions are failing many people. Through property investment you can provide a nest egg which will enable you to retire when you choose. How would you define retirement? Is it the age at which the government says you can retire? Does it mean stopping work altogether? I define retirement as:

> *"Living on an income which is not generated by your employment."*

This is known as "passive income" and it comes from income-producing assets such as property, shares, cash in the bank, or royalties. Of all income-producing assets, property is the most powerful.

You can retire on the day that your passive income exceeds your expenditure. Won't that be a wonderful day? You will get up when you want to, have breakfast and stroll down to the newsagents to pick up your paper. The sun will be shining and you will be on top of the world. This book is written to help you prepare for that day.

Pay off your mortgage early

The market can pay off your mortgage many times faster than you can. We bought our first house in 2003. It was a seller's market in those days and I didn't have a clue about property, so we paid the full asking price of £99,950. Incidentally, my brother-in-law had bought exactly the same type of house several years earlier for £16,000 under the local authority rent-right-to-buy scheme, but I couldn't think about that too much, as it made me ill! We had a mortgage of £75,000 on a repayment basis (interest plus capital) and the monthly payments were £410.76. At the time I was taking home £304.00 a week.

In 2007 the house was valued at £170,000. In that four-year period we paid off around £7,000 of the capital, leaving £68,000 on the mortgage. However the property had increased in value by at least £70,000, so the market had risen ten times faster than I could repay the mortgage! If I had been able to buy two properties in 2003 I could have sold the second one off in 2007 and paid the mortgage on my own house, leaving me mortgage-free in four years! In addition, if I had switched to an interest-only mortgage, I would have had a lower mortgage payment for those four years, plus some cash flow from my rental property.

Of course those were years of high growth in the property market. And it's true that in the early years you pay off more interest than capital on your mortgage. But it serves to illustrate that the market can work a lot harder than you can. Historically, house prices have doubled on average every seven to ten years, so it should not take more than this to pay off your mortgage.

Get on to the property ladder

You don't have to be a homeowner to become a landlord. You could buy a property in a less expensive part of the country as an investment, while renting your own accommodation close to your employment. When there is enough equity accumulated in the property, you can sell it and use this as a deposit for your own home. There are special deals and financing arrangements available to first time buyers. Take advantage of these to get your foot on the property ladder.

Neil Mansell explains how he began investing in property and became the owner of several HMO's (House of Multiple Occupancy) while still living in rented accommodation. He says, "The house that we bought in 2008 was much bigger, more expensive and nicer than we could have bought if I had jumped in a few years earlier."[ix]

Help your children onto the property ladder

In 2007 the average age of first time buyers in the UK was estimated to be thirty-three. This rose to around forty in 2012. The number of adults in the UK returning to live with their parents is now over three million, four times what it was in 1979. These are now known as the "boomerang generation." The average first time buyer now spends over £80,000 on rent over a sixteen year period before becoming a homeowner.

You can also use property investment to help your children get onto the property ladder sooner. You can do this by using some of the equity in your house to serve as a deposit for your children's first property. This need not cost you money each month as your son or daughter can pay the interest on your extra borrowing plus the interest on their mortgage. Together these will usually be less than the market rent.

Buy the house you need, not the house you think you can afford

When you are starting out, a one-bed flat is often all you need to be happy. When you are married with a growing family, especially when your children are nearly adults, even a three-bed house can feel a bit tight. I am a great believer in owning the house that suits your need at a given time. How can you afford to move up when you need to?

You can achieve this by switching to an interest-only mortgage. We have seen that the property market can pay off your mortgage more quickly than you can. This means that, by investing in buy-to-let properties, you can provide enough equity in time to pay off the mortgage on your own house. This will enable you to switch to an interest-only mortgage for your residence. As a result, the monthly repayments will be lower and you will be able to afford a bigger mortgage and buy the house you need.

Pay for university costs

Tuition fees are now £9,000 per year at many universities in England. Living costs can easily total £7,000 per year. It is estimated that an average student debt on leaving university will be in excess of £50,000. This represents a crippling debt with which to begin a working career. It will only serve to increase the age at which former students purchase their first home.

Some parents are now finding a way to reduce university costs. Instead of renting, they buy a property near their children's university. Their son or daughter occupies one of the rooms and they let out the other rooms to fellow students. If this is planned well, the collected rent pays the mortgage. If there is excess rent it can be put towards living costs. They can therefore have free accommodation for the family student and help with their living expenses.

The mistake such temporary landlords often make is to sell the property as soon as their child finishes his or her studies. It is better instead to keep the house as an investment and use the rental income to pay off the student loan. Or wait until the equity is sufficient to pay the debt off in a lump sum. Imagine your child leaving university with no debt and perhaps even a lump sum to put towards his or her first property. This is perfectly achievable and makes good sense.

Help a charity which is close to your heart

You may be involved with a charity in the UK or abroad. You could invest in a buy-to-let property and use the profit to provide regular funding for the charity. In addition, the property could be left to the charity in your will. They could sell it to fund a large project or use it to provide long-term funding. You could buy a property which can be used as an office by the charity. The Church of England is one of the largest property owners in the UK.

Leave a portfolio of

income producing properties.

Leave a legacy

Whenever I look around a stately home, such as Longleat or a National Trust property, I always ask the guides where the money came from to build such a fine house. I was told that Tyntesfield house near Bristol was built by the Gibbs family. They made their fortune from the import of guano, a fertiliser made from South American seabird droppings. You may not have a monopoly on bird poo and you may not be able to leave behind a sumptuous mansion, but it would be nice to think you could pass something on to following generations.

After the frantic years of work and child-raising you have a right to look forward to a peaceful retirement. Let us hope it is a long and happy one. We've been exploring ways that property can help you make it a more comfortable one. But have you thought about what you will leave to your children after you have gone? Ideally it's best to plan this so as to benefit them when they need it most, without impoverishing yourself in the short term. You could be sitting on an asset worth over £200,000, but if you live until you are ninety your children could be well into their sixties before they benefit from their inheritance. Another problem facing many people today is that their house has to be sold to pay for their nursing home care. Often very little is left to share out amongst the children.

Wouldn't it be more sensible to make provision for your children before this happens? You could help them onto the property ladder, or you could leave them a portfolio of income-producing properties. Property is different from a pension in this respect. When you buy an annuity with your pension pot you will receive an income for the rest of your life. But when you pass away the company keeps the money in most cases. However, property is yours to pass on to whomever you choose. It is an asset that is controlled by you, not some unknown fund manager. It is not a piece of paper, like a share certificate, which can lose most of its value in a very short time. Bricks and mortar can be seen and touched. A sound property investment will go on producing income long after you've gone.

The Luptons of Leeds were wealthy mill owners in the 19th century. Francis Lupton used the profits from the textile manufacturing business to build a large property empire. The property holdings stayed in the family, producing large amounts of rent. Mr. Lupton arranged for the family fortune to be placed in trusts. These were to be used specifically to fund the education of succeeding generations of the Lupton and Middleton families. This legacy allowed his descendant, Catherine Elizabeth Middleton, to attend St. Andrews University in Fife. There she met Prince William, and the rest you know.

I wonder what legacy you could leave?

Chapter Four

Four ways to profit from property

Why is property such a good investment? Because it offers several ways to make a profit. Most of all, property enables you to make use of a very powerful factor: the principle of leverage.

Buy at a discount and achieve instant equity

The first way to profit from property is to buy at less than the normal market value. This is commonly referred to as buying, *below market value* (BMV). You make a profit when you buy, not when you sell. This is especially true in a slow rising market. When you buy below market value you have built-in equity from the start.

You make a profit when you buy,

not when you sell.

Now you may ask why someone would sell their house or flat at a discount. You would be surprised to know that properties are sold every day for less than their full value. This is because property is sold on an open market. When you go into a department store or a supermarket to shop for food or clothes, you expect to pay the price marked on the tag. However, in an open market situation, an item is only worth what someone else is prepared to pay for it. Wholesalers buy their produce at a market where the price is determined by the quantity of produce available – supply – and the number of people who want to buy it – demand.

Prices in the property market are governed by the same principle. Many other factors come into play, such as property chains, buyer's income, and availability of finance; but the fundamental idea is the same.

You may say, isn't this cheating the seller out of the true value of his or her home? Well, everyone loves to find a bargain and you never worry about the shop owner's profit margin, do you? The price has to be agreed between the buyer and the vendor, and if you can meet the criteria, at a given time, that no one else can meet, you can make a deal and everyone will be happy.

To buy at a discount you need to find a situation where the vendor is willing to accept a lower price for his or her property. This could be for one of many reasons. Perhaps he or she has to move urgently to start a new job in another town. It could be that the property is run down and the owner cannot be bothered, or cannot afford, to renovate it. You might buy a repossessed property or an auctioned property. There may be an issue concerning a lease or other legal difficulties you can resolve. You could buy a property cheaply from a developer because they just want to get their money out quickly. There are also companies that reserve properties in bulk for investors and pass on the discounts obtained.

When we bought our first buy-to-let property, I was not an experienced negotiator. That is the thing about experience, until you do something, you will never have any. However, I managed to obtain a discount of £3,000 on the asking price. When the market is strong, as it was in the UK from 2002-2008, properties sell quickly. This is a vendor's market. It takes much more skill and speed to obtain a discount in these conditions. We will look at how to negotiate in chapter eight.

Since the credit crunch, however, a buyer has become a rarer creature. Consequently, someone who is keen to sell will be much more open to negotiation. In other words, it is a buyer's market. Just settle in your mind that if you have a deposit, and the required income, you will probably be able obtain a buy-to-let mortgage, even in today's difficult economic climate. You have no property to sell, so you are not in a chain. These factors put you in a strong negotiating position. They give you an opportunity to make a profit. Search carefully for a BMV property.

Improve the property and add value

The second way to make money from property is to increase its value. This is your chance to roll up your sleeves and get stuck in. If you are not very manual or you do not have the time, you could employ tradespeople to do it for you. The property may need just a lick of paint and some new carpets, or you may need to install a new kitchen or bathroom. If it comes to a new roof, doors and windows you need to be sure that the discount you obtained will not be cancelled out by the refurbishment costs!

You may be able to create another bedroom, or an additional bathroom, thus adding value. Some people may wish to sell the property at this point and take their profits. This is known as property development, rather than property investing. You need to decide from the beginning whether you want to be a property developer, or a property investor, as this will affect your financing arrangements.

I am always amazed at some people's lack of imagination when it comes to viewing a property. One couple may turn their noses up at a shabby house, but a person with imagination will be able to envisage the room as it will look after repainting and carpeting. The ability to see a house as it could look will give you an edge when it comes to buying. Be on the lookout for a house or flat whose shabbiness stands out in a smart area.

Make a profit from rental income

The golden rule of property investing is that the investment should not cost you money after the initial outlay. The deposit can even be returned to you after purchase, meaning that your investment can be practically free! More on this in chapter nine.

Property investment is a business. As all business people know, you have costs as part of the process, but as long as your costs are less than your income, you are in profit.

The formula for business.

Turnover less expenses = profit

The formula for property investing.

Rent less mortgage & costs – cash flow.

I emphasize this because you would be amazed at the number of people who buy a property that costs them money every month. A good investment will put money into your pocket every month, not take it out.

Many large businesses, with turnover in the tens of millions, operate at a loss for the first few years. In property investment it is quite possible to have a positive cash flow from the first month. Consider the following example.

Rent £700.00 – Mortgage & Costs £374.00 = Cash flow £326.00 = 46%

In case you are wondering, this is a real example. A profit margin like this also gives you a buffer against changes in market conditions and unforeseen expenses such as repairs and void periods. Good research and a grasp of the basic economics of property investment will help you find such investments.

Property investing can provide a regular source of income. It will pay you regularly, whether the sun is shining or it is raining. It will bring an income regardless of which government is in power. Your property is working for you seven days a week. Property even has an edge on owning a business. Your rental property does not call in sick, take a holiday or hand in its notice out of the blue. When properly managed, property will give you a regular second income to use as you please.

Your property is working for you

seven days a week.

Benefit from market rise

Property is a secure investment because it always increases in value. Not true, you say. Prices can also fall. Correct, but the general trend on a longer timescale is always upwards. Nationwide has published data on house prices since 1952.

Average UK house prices.
1952 £1,891
1962 £2,552
1972 £6,008
1982 £24,177
1992 £52,187
2002 £95,356
2011 £164,785

Since 1952 house prices have fallen on four occasions. In each case the drop in value was recovered within a few years. The average house price in the UK peaked in the third quarter of 2007 at £184,131. It fell to a low of £149,709 in 2009 but recovered to £164,785 in 2011. Prices have fallen around 11% from their peak in 2007. By contrast, interest rates on savings fell from 5.55% in 2007 to 3.5% in the first quarter of 2012, a fall of nearly 37%. House prices have more than doubled on average, every ten years. If this trend continues, the average house price in 2022 will be at least £325,000.

It is important to remember that these are national average house prices. Around the UK the picture is more varied. In some regions house prices have fallen further. In other areas, like parts of London and the south, house prices have continued to rise in spite of the recession.

Do you remember how much you paid for your first home? How much is it worth now? To give you a feel of the longer view, next time you visit your granny ask her how much she paid for her first house.

Take David – who bought his house in 1960. He paid £2,100 and his father told him he was mad because he would never be able to afford it. At the time David's weekly wage was £18.00 and the mortgage was £18.00 a month. His house is now worth around £180,000. In our day you can't buy any UK property for £2,100. It might just cover the fees! Unless fifty years of house price trends are going to change permanently, we can say that the value of property is set to continue rising.

Why do house prices keep going up?

Firstly, house prices keep rising because of inflation. The price of everything keeps going up. So your house will also continue to rise in value. By contrast, the mortgage debt on your investment property does not rise. This means that the equity in your house will increase.

Let's expand a little on the effects of inflation. Inflation is bad for the economy. But inflation is the friend of the property investor. Even if you only pay the interest on the mortgage, the comparative value of the debt is reduced every year by inflation. At the time of writing, the UK inflation rate stands at 3.4%. This means that your money in the bank is losing its purchasing power at a rate of 3.4% per year. Inflation erodes the value of savings but it has the reverse effect on debt. At the current rate your mortgage debt is decreasing in relative size by 3.4% annually. It is a debt, frozen in time, which is being eroded each year, until its value is only a fraction of what it was.

In the example of David's house, bought in 1960, the mortgage was £1,890. This is a small sum compared to mortgages today. Yet the monthly repayment was nearly a quarter of his wage at the time. So our mortgages today, which seem huge, will appear cheap in years to come.

House prices will also continue to rise because of the housing shortage. Remember the principle of supply and demand? People may be able to do without the latest gadget or luxury, but everyone needs a roof over their head. In the UK we live on an island with limited space and a growing population. The population density in England is among the highest in Europe.

Inflation is the friend

of the property investor.

Tom de Castella writes, "Just 134,000 new homes were built in the UK in 2010 – the lowest number since World War II. This is despite 230,000 new households being formed every year. By 2025 there will be a housing shortfall of 750,000 in England alone, according to the IPPR."[x]

The market fundamentals are strong. So, while no-one can predict the future, the likelihood is that house prices will continue to rise. This means that your investment will give you a very good return.

On a regional level, house prices rise due to local economic and social factors. If several companies move into an area and offer good wages, property nearby becomes more desirable. Higher prices are more affordable to high wage earners. A new school can attract young families into an area, driving up house prices. A large investment in infrastructure or local amenities can have the same effect.

So you can see that property can offer at least four ways to make a profit. Compare this with an investment in stocks and shares. Provided the share price rises, you can benefit in two ways, by the value of the share rising and by receiving a dividend.

Now I want to show you property's ace card.

Leverage – the magic multiplier

The principle of leverage is a very clever aspect of property investment. Leverage allows you to control a large asset with a small amount of your own cash. You gain capital appreciation on the total value of the asset, using the bank's money.

Let us take a fictional example. Jane wants to buy a house worth £100,000. She has to put down a deposit, which we'll say is £25,000. She can then obtain a buy-to-let mortgage from the bank for the other £75,000 of the value. She now legally owns an asset worth £100,000. If she were to leave her £25,000 in the bank at an interest rate of 3.5%, she would achieve a return of £875 in 12 months. However, when her money is invested in property and the market rises by 3.5% that same year her return would be £3,500. The market rise is applied to the full value of the property, not just to her deposit. This is the principle of leverage. It can permit you to quadruple the return on your investment.

The principle of leverage
can quadruple your return.

I hope by now you are beginning to see the advantages of property investment over pensions and other forms of investment such as stocks and shares. However, I am aware that many objections and fears often come to mind. These can deter you from making a start. In the next chapter I want to take time to look at some of the most common reasons why people are hesitant to put their money into bricks and mortar.

Chapter Five

What's stopping you?

In this chapter we'll look at common obstacles and objections stopping people from launching into property investment. You may identify with some of these, or you may have others not mentioned here. We will discuss each difficulty in turn and suggest that the main underlying emotion is usually fear.

I don't have any money.

Contrary to what some property investment gurus may have been teaching, you do need money to invest in property. There may have been a time when, through clever strategies and creative financing, it was possible to buy property with no deposit money. However, things have changed and elaborate forms of financing have become more difficult to put together. Those times could yet return, as no one can predict the future.

For the moment, however, just resolve to build up a reserve of money for the purpose of property investment. The biggest amount will be for the deposit. Then there are legal fees, survey and other costs. The amount will vary across the country. To invest in property in Bristol, you will need at least £20,000 – £30,000.

You could be sitting on
more money than you need.

The creativity comes in the way you raise the money. When I first began to look into property investment in 2007, I thought I would have to save up a lot of money before I could get started. However, I was about to find out that I already had all the money I needed.

I had a customer who had called me three or four times in the space of two years to ask me to check out the electrics in the houses he had just bought. After the third one I got curious and asked him "Are you a millionaire? How do you buy all these houses?" He explained how he had used the equity from his home as a deposit for his first investment, a three-bedroom house. He then re-mortgaged the second house to provide a deposit for the next one.

He asked how much equity we had in our house. I realised that we had over £100,000. His eyes lit up and he exclaimed, "You don't need to save up, you are sitting on more money than you need to fund a property investment".

So raising capital through additional borrowing on your existing mortgage is one way to finance property investment. Please note that this is not the same as an equity release scheme where you sign over your house to a company in exchange for a cash payment. Re-mortgaging or additional borrowing means that you remain the sole owner of your property.

Alternatively, you might have savings or investments in stocks and shares that could give you a better return if invested in property. You might inherit a sum of money.

If money is tight, you can make the most of your available time to learn about property investment and take the DIY approach. You can use your time to do viewings and to do much of the refurbishing work yourself. You could learn all about property investment and do a joint venture with someone else who has money, but no time or knowledge.

Case study – Andrew

I began investing in property when I reached my forties and discovered that I had left it too late to build up a pension. My profession as a surveyor had taught me a great deal about property. I knew that in the long term property outperforms all other asset classes. Furthermore you can leverage it in the form of bank loans in a way that you cannot do with stocks and shares.

My inspiration was my investment partner. One day he said I should get off my backside and go and buy something instead of just talking about it. So we took out a bank loan and purchased our first property together. I later bought more property with my business partner and I now have three joint venture partners.

The main difficulty I have encountered over the years is raising finance. Banks will lend more readily for development projects, because you are making a short-term profit. At least this was the case before the credit crunch. It is harder to keep re- mortgaging properties to raise new deposits. I find we have to put more money into the pot to keep moving forward.

I have watched my portfolio grow over the years. In these times of low interest rates there is a real income generated by the rents. Of course we are re-investing this, as it is after all my pension. I now have something I didn't have when I started, which is real value in my properties. Hopefully this will produce an income for me when I retire. I am not there yet. I probably need to double what I have now in order to be able to buy a good annuity without having to sell the properties.

My exit strategy is to form some kind of holding company and to pass the properties on to my children through it. I want to build up my portfolio and keep the properties long term. I am putting the right infrastructure in place, such as boilers and good kitchens, to make the maintenance easy when I retire.

My top tip for new investors is to learn all you can. Understand the market as well as possible. Do not risk it all yourself if you are a complete beginner, but do a joint venture with someone who has some experience. Two brains are better than one in this game. That way if you do catch a cold, it will be halved, rather than taking the hit all by yourself. It is very important for your first two or three investments to get it right. It pays to do your homework.

Then there is always good old fashioned saving. If you decide to tie your money up for three years you could get a better interest rate on your savings. As an illustration, if you began with a lump sum of £5,000 and made a monthly deposit of £400, with 4.5% monthly compounded interest, after three years this would become £21,125. Could you find a way to make this happen?

Top tip: There are many ways to fund a property investment.

I don't have the time.

Time is never found; it has to be made. There is usually a trade-off of time against money. If you have no time, it may be because you have a demanding job. However this job may provide you with a good income. If your job is very time consuming and family commitments prevent you from spending time on property investment, there is always the option of using others to do the leg work for you.

Property investment experts can be employed for your benefit. There are a range of services offered by companies of varying competence and value. There are companies who source property deals. Others can help you find a tenant and manage your property. Some offer a complete service, helping you to buy the right property in the right place, to find a tenant and to manage the letting. They may even carry out a yearly review to help you grow your portfolio. We will look more closely at the property investment service industry later.

Time is never found,

it has to be made.

When I started taking time off work to view properties I was tempted to think that I was losing money and would be better off sticking to my job. The thing to remember about property investment is that it provides what is called, *passive income*. So time invested at the onset provides a return for years to come.

Top tip: Use other people's knowledge and skills to build your property portfolio.

It's not the right time to buy.

Does anyone really know when the right time to buy is? When house prices are falling, first time buyers will typically wait for the market to fall further. When prices are rising, they rush to buy before houses become too expensive. This influx of buyers drives property prices even higher. The real question is not when to buy, but how and where. As we have seen, you need to buy at a discount. We'll speak later about the importance of researching the right location.

We bought our first investment property at the height of the property boom in 2007. Because we did our homework and bought a property capable of achieving a positive cash flow, it was still a good investment. Today, despite being in negative equity, this property is more profitable than ever, because of low interest rates.

The market is always going to have ups and downs. Usually one negative factor will be compensated by a positive one elsewhere. Since the credit crunch in 2008, property prices have fallen by between 10-15% in some parts of the UK. However, rental demand is strong. This means that now is a pretty good time to buy. House prices and other factors will always fluctuate, so if you are waiting for the perfect time to buy, you could wait a long time.

Top tip: Don't wait to buy property, buy property and wait.

Now is a pretty good time to buy.

Landlords are all greedy, nasty people aren't they?

The short answer is "No." There are good landlords and bad landlords and it is up to you to decide what kind of landlord you want to be. There will always be a need for affordable, well maintained properties, so being a good landlord is best for both tenant and investor.

Landlords probably got a bad name due to the unscrupulous activities of a few notorious landlords after the war when houses were in short supply. The Rent Act of 1957 was passed to curb these abuses. This legislation made being a landlord unattractive to investors because they found it difficult to evict problem tenants. The Housing Acts of 1988 and 1996 were designed to redress the balance, and now both tenants and landlords have rights and protection. The most important legal document for tenants and landlords is the Assured Shorthold Tenancy agreement (AST).

When I first began looking into buy-to-let, I asked an agent to show me some properties. I was shown several houses and flats near the city centre. Some of the rooms were like rabbit hutches crowded with asylum-seeker tenants. It was at that point that I decided that if I was going to be a landlord, I would have to be able to stand in front of a property and not be ashamed to say it was mine.

Landlords are still often treated with disdain in the media. However, the simple fact is that without private landlords there would not be enough properties for rent in the UK. In 2012 private rentals made up around 16% of the UK housing market, up from 11% in 2003. Council housing accounts for another 17%. Owner-occupied homes make up 67%, down from 71% in 2003. So the trend is towards renting. As the government has not been building many council houses over the past 20 years, there is a dependence on the private rental-sector to provide homes for rent. A shortage of rental properties injures the economy, as people cannot move to new areas to find work. So, despite the bad press that buy-to-let landlords often receive, they are an essential part of the UK economy.

Top tip: Property investors play an important role in the economy.

My money is safer in the bank

Are you sure about that? The annual rate of inflation is currently 3.2%. If your cash is only earning 2.5% interest, then it is depreciating in value. Those who are perhaps hardest hit by the credit crunch are the people who have worked hard all their lives and saved up for their retirement. Someone with £40,000 in savings in 1987 would have been able to achieve an annual interest of £4,216.00. In 2011 this same amount produced only £1,100. This reflects the 2011 average interest rate on savings of 2.75%.[xi] By contrast, for most of 2011 the rate of inflation was over 5%. This means that, in real terms, your money is losing value every passing day.

Learn the difference between

good debt and bad debt.

People sometimes refer to property as a risky investment. However when you consider the alternatives, such as investing in stocks and shares, in business, or leaving your money in the bank, you might conclude that it's more risky to neglect property investment.

Top tip: Protect your money against inflation and low interest rates by investing in property.

I don't want to be in debt

That's a good thing. However it is important to know the difference between good debt and bad debt. Bad debt is incurred to acquire depreciating commodities such as cars, clothes and gadgets. Good debt is incurred to purchase assets that will increase in value, like a successful business or a property. The entire business world operates on this principle. If you are a homeowner you probably needed a mortgage to buy your house. So you have to agree that not all debt is bad.

We all accept that credit cards and loans have been used to excess in our society in recent years. However, credit can be very useful if used correctly and not abused. When you borrow money to make money that is good business.

Top tip: Learn the difference between good debt and bad debt.

What if I can't find a tenant?

There is an acute housing shortage in the UK. As a result, rental demand is very high and is set to remain so due to the low number of houses being built. At the height of the property boom a serious problem for house buyers was gazumping. Now, in some areas, gazumping is taking place among prospective tenants! This is not the case in all areas, however, so it is important to buy a house in an area with a high rental demand. This is where good research comes in. It will show you where to buy a property for maximum occupancy.

Top tip: Do your research well and buy a property which will rent out easily.

What if I get the tenant from hell?

As a landlord, I've found that it's important to have some faith in human nature. There are good and bad people out there. The vast majority are good. But only the bad ones make the headlines in most cases.

Our very first tenant was a young girl who was signed up for us by a letting agent. We met her for the first time the day she moved in. I was now a landlord! How does a landlord speak and act I wondered? This was the beginning of a new role for me. We exchanged a few awkward pleasantries. I showed her how the boiler worked and nervously gave her the keys. Then I left with my fingers crossed.

The first month's rent was paid up front, so no worries. I eagerly scanned the bank statements to check that month number two would be paid. It was. By this time, buoyed by our success, we were planning to move to a larger house and rent out our existing home (this is called a let-to-buy). We did several viewings and put an offer in for a house.

One morning I had a call from the estate agent while at work, to say our offer had been accepted. Elated by this news, I was in high spirits. I climbed my steps to install a light for a customer. Then the telephone rang. It was my tenant. Could she pay a bit late this month as she had spent a lot at Christmas and could not afford the rent? I felt my heart sink from the top of the steps right to the floor! Disaster! What to do? How to cope?

I felt my heart sink

right to the floor.

She left the house soon afterwards and we found a new tenant fairly quickly. And just to prove that we need faith in human nature, her family sent us £20 per week until all the arrears were repaid.

This story shows that one of the key factors in finding a good tenant is to first find a good letting agent. Because I was using the tenant finding service and not the full management service, my agent was not concerned about the long-term affordability for the young person. He just took his commission and disappeared, leaving me to sort out the headache.

I cannot promise that you will never have a troublesome tenant. But if you follow the proper procedures, such as credit checks and tenancy deposits, you will have some protection against the worst scenarios. You can also buy a rent guarantee for a tenant who passes the referencing process. If you advertise the property yourself, spend some time speaking with a prospective tenant. You can usually assess the measure of a person in this way. Ask for a reference from their former landlord. If you use an agent, make sure they work with integrity.

Top tip: Use credit referencing and rent guarantees to minimise tenant problems.

I can't be bothered fixing toilets

The good news is you don't have to. Fortunately handymen and plumbers exist to take care of all this. Here is a key point in property investment: you have to move from a DIY mentality to a Project Manager mentality. The costs are covered by your rental profit. A proper budget for buy-to-let will include an allowance for repairs and maintenance.

I know the feeling though. You buy a house that needs some work and think to yourself, "I will just do it myself over time." But time is the one thing you are short of. And when you have the time it seems you are always short of money. We took five years to do up our first house and that was without major refurbishment. You may have been planning work on your house for years. Then to think you will have to do it all again for the benefit of others – it can be just exhausting!

Many people since the credit crunch have become "accidental landlords." That is, they have been unable to sell their homes so they have moved to a new house and rented out their old one. I spoke with one such couple who were complaining about their bad tenants. The tenants had stopped paying the rent. It transpired, however, that they had been very slow to have the boiler repaired in the middle of winter. They ended up in court. This is simply not good business. You have to remember that the property is your asset. Keeping it in good repair will maintain its value as well as ensuring you have happy tenants.

Top tip: Build a support network to help maintain your properties.

My partner is too afraid

This is a big one. You may be convinced that property investment is sensible and worthwhile. Your wife, husband or partner may not agree. This is the case for many people. It was the case for us. I had been doing research for six months. I read several books and spoke to people who were involved in buy-to-let. I did some number crunching, comparing property investment to other forms of saving and pension schemes. It made sense to me to invest in property. Ruth was not so sure.

I started viewing properties, looking for an investment that stacked up. I found a property I calculated would earn us £75.00 per month. So I put in an offer and after some negotiation my increased offer was accepted. Then I came home and announced, "I've just bought a house." Ruth went ballistic!

We had words and she reproached me for not including her in the decision. I said it was me who was going to have to work until I was sixty-seven to pay off the mortgage, so I felt it was my call. This remained a sore point for some time, especially when we started to have problems with tenants. However, within eight months we had moved to a larger house thanks to the principles of property investment. Ruth eventually started to see the advantages and came round to the same way of thinking. For my part, I recognised that I should have taken her with me on the learning journey from the beginning.

My wife went ballistic!

Ruth's story

My parents were on a low income and could never afford a house of their own. We were council tenants. So I had never been used to owning my own home. When I was working as an enrolled nurse, I looked into buying a flat. I even saw one I liked and made an offer. But someone else outbid me. When we bought our first home I was confident we could afford the mortgage. But the thought of owning more houses scared me.

Since we have been investing in property I have learned a lot. Now I know I could have taken in a lodger to help pay the mortgage back then, but I never thought of it at the time. I think fear comes from a lack of knowledge. My way of thinking needed to be changed through education and understanding. It's all about cash flow. When you see how it works, your mentality changes.

Your situation may be different. Only you can address this issue, together with your partner.

Top tip: Make the learning journey together.

The underlying reason is fear

In her excellent book *Feel the Fear and Do It Anyway,* Susan Jeffers explains that we all feel fear when we leave our comfort zone. However, as soon as you do, the comfort zone enlarges and the fear subsides.

The day I picked up the keys from the estate agent and went to look over our first investment property I was way outside my comfort zone. I was so nervous that I found it hard to concentrate. After doing some work on the house, I drove off and left my toolbox in the garden. By the time I returned it had been stolen! Five years later, investing in property is well within my comfort zone. Writing this book is my new comfort zone challenge!

Knowledge reduces fear.

I read an article many years ago entitled *"FOF and FOP."* Fear of failure and fear of people can prevent you from doing so many things. You have to ask yourself who you have been listening to. Your friends or work colleagues may have friendly advice to offer, but do they know the principles of property investment? It is best to take advice from someone who has been there and done it. The answer lies in learning more about how property can help you prepare for the future.

Top tip: Fear grows in the absence of knowledge. Therefore knowledge reduces fear and brings it to a manageable level.

Chapter Six

Where do I begin?

If you have read this far, you may at least be curious about how to invest in property. That is a good place to start. In this chapter we'll look at how to do the groundwork for a successful investment. We will begin with education. Developing a business mind-set is the key to success. Growing your mind will enable you to grow your portfolio. We will also look at getting financially in shape and setting some goals.

Understand the nature of investment

You need to grasp the principle of investment in order to profit from property. The basic idea of investment is to put something in, in order to get more out at a later stage. We have been raised in a consumer society, where people earn and spend, earn and spend. This mind-set has to change to earn, invest, and then spend.

A farmer invests when he plants a seed in the ground. He foregoes the immediate benefit of eating the seed in the hope of a bigger return when harvest comes. We all invest, in the broadest sense, every day. We buy good food, fruit and veg, to invest in our health. We buy fashionable clothes to feel good about our appearance.

Investment often requires us to borrow money. A student will borrow to invest in a good education. The objective is to land a highly paid job that will enable him or her to pay back the loan and build a comfortable lifestyle.

Investment is essential in the business world. A company must borrow to build a factory and equip it with machinery. It may be several years before this capital outlay is returned. Then more investment will be needed for growth. In the UK, there has been a lack of investment in infrastructure. The water network in England and Wales loses 3.36 billion litres of water a day because the pipes are old and leaking. In some areas, traffic bottlenecks often cause haulage firms to miss their delivery targets. Without investment, the nation would eventually grind to a halt.

Delayed gratification is a fundamental principle of investing. An experiment devised by Stanford University in the 1960's became famous as an illustration of this principle. Children were asked in turn to sit alone in a room in front of a table. A marshmallow was then placed on the table. The researcher explained that he was going to leave the room for a while and he gave each child a choice: either eat the marshmallow now, or wait until he returned in which case they could have two marshmallows. The experiment was originally conceived to understand at what age the concept of deferred gratification develops in children. An unexpected result emerged however, as time went by. Researchers discovered that the children who were able to delay gratification achieved greater success in life.

Understand the principle of delayed gratification.

When you set your property investment goals, you may need to put off some short-term projects like a new kitchen or a bigger car, to save up your first deposit. Just keep in mind that in the long run you will be able to afford a nicer kitchen or better car.

Robert Kiyosaki's book, *"Rich Dad, Poor Dad,"* is a great introduction to investing. Kiyosaki tells the story of his own father and his friend's father who each had a different approach to their career. Mr. Kiyosaki senior chose to become a teacher and rose to become head of the department of education in the state of Hawaii. The friend's dad came from a poor background, but he started several small businesses and worked to build them up. When Kiyosaki returned from the Marines several years later, his own father had lost his job and all the benefits that went with it. His friend's father, on the other hand, was just completing the purchase of a beachfront apartment block, thanks to his businesses and investments. *Rich Dad, Poor Dad* is a plea to whoever will listen, not to rely solely on employment for a secure financial future. Investing is the real way to prosper.

Learn about property investment

To be able to make a good investment it is essential that you learn the rules of the craft. You would not think of driving a car without first learning the Highway Code. And I would not trust a surgeon who just turned up at the hospital and said he would just make a start and see how things went! Strangely though, some people seem to approach property investment with this attitude. A certain amount of research is needed before you can be sure of making a good investment. Even if you use the services of a property investment expert, it is good to know what to expect from him.

When I first began considering property investing I searched for relevant books on Amazon, including, *Successful Property Letting* by David Lawrenson. I learned from people who had done it before and got some feel for the process. I spoke to letting agents to find out which type of property was renting well in their area. I tried some tests on the rental market to check demand in various areas. After six months I made my first investment. After that first experience I continued to learn, attending seminars and networking events. The learning process will continue as your portfolio grows. No one knows it all. I certainly don't. I'm learning all the time.

Develop a business mind-set

If you are new to property investment, and especially if you don't run your own business, your thinking will have to change. You will need to develop a "can do" mind-set. This involves being optimistic. Along the way you will run into problems. A problem solving mind-set will enable you to find solutions. Property investment is a business and you need to approach it as such for best results.

At an early stage you need to assess your attitude to risk. Are you risk averse or adventurous by nature? Either way you can still invest in property. You can do it the ultra-safe way, with the help of professionals. Or you can try more risky, arguably more profitable, ways of going about it.

What is your attitude to loss? I read an interesting statement once about losing money. Someone said they knew poor people who have never lost money, but they could not think of any rich people who had never lost money. We have lost money while investing in property. On two occasions a vendor has pulled out of a sale and we have lost several hundred pounds in fees. How would you feel if that happened? You have to keep your eyes on the big picture. You have to tell yourself that you may be able to make up the loss on the next purchase. If you cannot bear to lose money you will be stuck in a frugal mind-set.

Read about the careers of Richard Branson, Duncan Bannatyne and others who started small and built up their businesses. Attend a seminar by a successful entrepreneur. Be inspired. In 2009 I attended a weekend of training with property investor and entrepreneur Kevin Green. What an inspiration! My mind was buzzing with ideas for days afterwards. This led to an expansion in our business. Kevin speaks regularly at training events for entrepreneurs across the country.

You have to break out of the mind-set where you expect your employer or the state to look after you. It may not happen. This has to sink in. Take control of your own future. Be your own boss.

Take control of your future.

Assess your strengths and weaknesses

What are you good at? What skills and abilities can you bring to your new investment business? Are you good at administration? Can you paint and fix things? Do you have flexible working hours? Make an inventory of your strengths and see how these can help you.

What do you hate doing? Think about the areas where you will need help. Are you frustrated because you have no time to get started? Use others to fill in your areas of weakness.

Establish your budget

Do you know how much you are spending each month? Do you have any disposable income? In Annexe 1 I have included an Excel spread sheet to help you work out your total outgoings, if you have not already done so. Compare this to your income and you will see how much you will be able to save towards investing. Apply the principle of delayed gratification to your spending. Controlling your budget is important. Some people in their enthusiasm to grow a large portfolio have overstretched themselves, and have lost the lot when things went wrong.

Many people ask whether they should pay off their debts before investing in property. Personally I believe it is preferable to do both simultaneously. If you have credit card debt, make a plan to pay down the balance on credit cards with the highest interest rate first. Alternatively, you can transfer a balance to a card with zero interest for a set period. At the same time begin to set funds aside for your deposit. Remember that property is a great means of wealth creation. When you make money from a good investment, you can pay off your debt in one go. I hasten to add that I am not a financial advisor and I offer this purely as a personal opinion.

Work out your personal pension deficit

Do you know what date your state pension will begin? You may find it's now going to be later than you thought. Ask the Department for Work and Pensions for a pension forecast. Do you have other pensions? How much income will these produce? Consider putting all your pensions into one pot. You can then take advice on how to make this work as hard as possible for you. Ask a financial advisor for a review of your pension arrangements. Then obtain a forecast of how much you can expect to receive when you retire. Do you have any other assets or investments that will produce passive income? Add up all your expected retirement income.

Next, look at your expenses again and try to estimate how much you will need to have coming in when you are no longer working. You may have paid off your mortgage and other loans by then, so these can be subtracted. However, food and utilities may cost more in the future. Include a budget for any extras you would like to enjoy such as travel, or treating the grandchildren.

These exercises will give you two figures. This will tell you whether you can expect a pension surplus or a pension deficit. You may be alarmed to find there is a significant shortfall. Better to find out now than at age sixty-eight. This realisation may give you the motivation you need to get started. (You will find additional information in Annexe 1 to help you work out your pension deficit.)

Obtain a copy of your credit report

Did you know there are credit files held on you by three separate credit-referencing agencies in the UK? Everyone has a credit file, unless, of course, you have never borrowed money. Every time you take out a credit card, a loan, or pay for goods in several instalments, a note goes on your credit file. Some people have hardly ever borrowed money, so their file is very thin. However this isn't to your advantage. When you apply for a buy-to-let mortgage, the lender wants to see a history of borrowing and repaying credit. This confirms your track record as a responsible borrower. Banks want to be confident you will repay the money they lend you. You don't have an automatic right to credit.

You can obtain a copy of your credit report from www.checkmyfile.com This website will give you access to the reports of all three credit referencing agencies. These reports also give you a credit score. If your score is low, there are ways to increase it.

See www.moneysavingexpert.com for excellent tips on how to do this.

Get your finance in place

Ask a local estate agent to value your home. Then find out from your existing mortgage provider how much remains to be paid on your mortgage. This will show how much equity you have. Find a good mortgage broker and ask for a pre-investment assessment. You will need to bring along your household budget, proof of income and proof of deposit. The broker can then advise you on what you will be able to borrow. This will help you to target your research on properties suitable to your budget. Aiming too high can overstretch your finances. Equally, you could miss out on higher returns if you do not know what you can afford.

Ask your broker to request an agreement in principle from a buy-to-let lender. You will appear more professional if you can approach an estate agent and say that you have a deposit in place and your broker has pre-qualified you for a mortgage. As we'll see in chapter seven, many estate agents will invite you to speak to their in-house mortgage adviser. You can do this just to humour them, but don't give too much away.

These steps will help you be well prepared for your first buy-to-let project. In chapter eight we'll take you through the complete investment process. But first a tour of the various professional services available to investors.

Chapter Seven

The buy-to-let service industry

Property investing is a team sport. It is important to know that you do not have to do everything on your own. Investing can be as hands-on or at arm's-length as you choose. This will depend on your budget, your skills and your aptitude. You can make use of the large and growing property investment service industry that has grown up in the last fifteen to twenty years.

Professional services

Firstly, of course, there are the professionals whose help you will need during the purchasing process: estate agents, auctioneers, solicitors and mortgage brokers. Let us look at these briefly.

Estate agents

Estate agents used to get bad press for not always describing a property accurately. "Deceptively spacious" meant you couldn't swing a cat in the room. "Requires some updating" was code for falling apart. In spite of this image, most are good at what they do. They usually have an accurate idea of how much a property is worth. Strangely though, estate agents do not always understand how property investment works. I have not met many who have a buy-to-let portfolio. Consequently they do not always know which properties are best suited for the investor. I have had agents show me properties that did not stack up in terms of affordability. So don't expect them to always give you the best advice.

It is important to register your interest in property with estate agents in your chosen area. Tell them the type of property you are looking for and ask to be put on their mailing list.

Case study – Ian

Going professional

I have been involved in the property business for over thirty years. I started an estate agency in Bristol and built it up to four branches, employing over forty staff. However, all this lost its meaning for me when my mother died suddenly in 1999 aged 59.

The shock made me realise that the most important thing in life is family. As a result I made some radical changes.

I sold my business and got a divorce. I found myself with a lump sum of £86,000. Many of my friends were investing in property and were doing very well. Of course, I knew the property market inside out, so I decided to invest myself. I bought four properties with my initial capital. These quickly grew in value and I used the equity that was created to continue to invest. I built a portfolio of twenty-three properties between 2001-2007.

Retiring at forty thanks to my property income, I spent six years in Spain enjoying life. However, after a while I decided that doing nothing was boring and I was too young to retire. By this time I was helping friends and family to invest in property, so I hit on the idea of doing this as a business. In 2008 I started Midas Estates, bringing together a team of property professionals to help other people build a sound portfolio.

For me the most important thing in property investing is choosing the right location. Thanks to my experience, I've always focused on this and as a result I have never had any voids.

I am remarried now and we are starting a family. I love to be able to choose when to work and this means I can spend more time with my loved ones.

My top tip for investors is to buy property in the right location. Take your time, be relaxed and enjoy building your portfolio.

Solicitors

Your solicitor is essential to the purchase process. People can sometimes be timid when it comes to dealing with professionals. We tend to accept what they say without question. However they are human, and have been known to make mistakes. My solicitor spotted an anomaly in the paperwork of a flat we were planning to buy. The lease was in fact illegal. Other solicitors had not detected the problem even though the property had been sold before. So you will need to find a good solicitor, as all are not the same.

Make sure your solicitor keeps you informed of the purchasing process and up-to-date on which party is holding up the sale. Don't be afraid to call them if you have not had any news for a while. With some solicitors things have a tendency to get done after a call from the client.

Mortgage brokers

You will also need a good mortgage broker. A mortgage broker is not the same as a mortgage adviser. A broker is independent and has access to the whole lending market. Advisers who work with estate agents may only be able to access the products of a few lenders.

When you approach an estate agent and ask to view a property you may be invited to have a chat with their mortgage adviser. I was once told that I could not do a viewing until I had done so. These are heavy sales tactics. The company might earn commission on deals arranged by their adviser, so they may not give you impartial advice. In my view there is also a conflict of interest here, as you don't really want the vendor's agent to know all about your financial situation. This can influence the negotiation process in their favour. Don't get locked-in to an adviser who has a limited number of products to choose from. Choose a broker who can give you a wider choice.

These days you can search online for a mortgage on price comparison sites. However, these sites are very robotic. They will give you a yes or no decision, without taking into account all of your circumstances. When we bought our house in 2008 our broker worked very hard on our behalf. She took our case to an independent underwriter and helped us to get a mortgage we might not otherwise have obtained. Some mortgage advisors can sell you the product that gives them the highest commission. It is best to use an Independent Mortgage Broker whom you trust.

Property auctions

The auctioneer is there to bring sellers and buyers together. This is the property market at its most dynamic expression. Buying at auction can be tricky as you are expected to do all your research up front without knowing whether or not you will win the auction. The savvy investor can pick up a bargain here. But you can also get carried away and pay more than you should. I would recommend doing plenty of research on the properties that interest you before buying at auction.

I attended an auction once and began chatting with a young man before the start of proceedings. He said he was accompanying his uncle who had a bungalow for sale in the auction. When the lot came up, who should start bidding for it but the uncle! Beware of vendors bidding to push up the price of the property. The auctioneer himself can also bid for the vendor in certain circumstances. Ask someone who is well acquainted with auctions to fill you in on the form. Try a dummy run before rushing in and paying over the odds.

Letting agents

Someone has said that 70% of letting agents are doughnuts! I have no way of verifying that, but I have certainly found some who fall short. We've also found ones who have provided an excellent service. A good letting agent will take a great deal of the stress out of being a landlord. So how do you find a good one? Try to find other landlords who have used an agent before and ask what they thought of the service. Personal recommendation is usually best. You could email your details to several agents and only consider those who get back to you within two days.

70% of letting agents are doughnuts.

Letting agents provide a service on various levels according to your requirements. The first level is the tenant finding service. For a set fee the agent will advertise your property, conduct viewings and set up the tenancy agreement. Under this arrangement you manage the property yourself from that point. The next level is a management service. This will also include rent collection, dealing with maintenance issues and managing deposits. Call in to a few agents' offices and ask for their lettings brochure.

Remember that the agent is working for you, not for the tenant. As some agents also charge tenants for their services, you can get the impression that you are the one being held to account. Letting agents are not regulated by government legislation, so some of the terms in their brochures are not legally binding. They just make them up. When you are told, for example, that you have to pay a further 5% after 12 months to renew the AST of a sitting tenant you can refuse. Just ask for this clause to be crossed off the contract. This and other points, such as exclusivity periods, can be negotiated with the agent. Don't forget, you are a businessperson now, so don't let them treat you like an amateur.

There are some good books on letting that provide a lot more information. You will find details in the back of this book, under Further Reading.

Credit referencing companies

It is essential to carry out a credit check on a potential tenant. A special licence is required for this. Letting agents employ a licensed company to carry out these checks. There are now several companies who offer this service directly to the landlord. You can obtain the forms from their website.

Inventory companies

A detailed inventory of the fixtures and fittings of the property must be carried out on the day the tenant enters the property. This will serve as proof to establish whether any damage has been done during the tenancy, beyond normal wear and tear. Photographic and video inventories are now often used. You can employ a specialised company for this. Without a proper inventory you will be unable to claim for damages to the property.

Tenancy deposit registration

The incoming tenant must pay a deposit equivalent to one month's rent to the landlord. This money must then be deposited with a registered organisation such as the Deposit Protection Service (DPS). At the end of the tenancy an inspection of the property will be carried out by the landlord in the presence of the tenant. Any damages should be noted and a sum agreed for the repair. The landlord will then inform the agency of the amount he is claiming. Any dispute is adjudicated by the agency. A detailed inventory and photos are essential to support the landlord's case.

Energy Assessors

All properties sold or rented out must have an Energy Performance Certificate (EPC). The estate agent will probably know an energy assessor who can produce one for you.

Insurance brokers

When you complete the purchase of your investment property you must have landlord's insurance in place. An insurance broker will find you the best price for this.

Accountants

You may also need the services of an accountant to help with your tax return. He can offer advice on minimising your tax liability by showing you what expenses you can deduct from your rental profits. An accountant can also help you with forward planning, which we'll speak about in chapter ten. Make sure your accountant is well versed in property tax planning.

Builders and handypersons

If your property requires some refurbishment before letting, you may need to employ tradespeople. Keep your builder up-to- date with the purchase process and let him know when you are due to exchange contracts. Try to ensure he will be available as soon as you have the keys. Agree a detailed schedule of works in advance, and be clear about what is included and what it will cost. Check whether the builder will arrange other trades such as electrician or plumber, or whether you have to do this. Visit the property regularly during the work to check on progress.

Training courses and property investment companies

The buy-to-let mortgage has only been around since the mid-nineties. It helped fuel a boom in the buy-to-let market, especially between 2002 and 2007. Where there is a market, a service industry will always grow up beside it. There are now a multitude of companies offering property investment training, coaching, property deal sourcing, and other services. Many of these offer sound advice and assistance. Some may be less reliable. All will offer their services for a fee.

Property investment seminars

Some people who have succeeded in property investment decide to share the secrets of their success with others. This type of education often begins with a free seminar at which you can learn useful information. The evening usually serves as a sales pitch for an advanced training package. Unlike mainstream education, the emphasis is put on building a mind-set and taking action. If you are a proactive person and you want to go far in property investment, then you can benefit from such training. The cost can be considered as an investment in your education.

A word of caution though; there can be a sense of inspiration and euphoria at such events when you are presented with the possibility of becoming wealthy. There are people who become addicted to this adrenalin rush and they become conference junkies. The vast majority of the trainees do not follow up with the action needed to achieve success. So just ask yourself if you will really benefit from this training. Be sure also to check out the credentials of the training company.

Some people become
conference junkies.

Kevin Green – Wealth Training.

Kevin Green is a self-made multi-millionaire and social entrepreneur. The former farmer, who is dyslexic, has featured on Channel 4's Secret Millionaire. In 1984 he was homeless; today his portfolio runs into the hundreds of properties. He has a wealth of experience in the property investment world and heads a number of successful companies and other non-property related businesses.

Kevin's desire now is to give back to the next generation of entrepreneurs by sharing his knowledge and wisdom. His speciality talks include motivation, empowerment and coaching and he enjoys giving businesses and organisations an insight into what it takes to become successful in the business world.

Kevin and his team invite you to attend a 2-day Wealth Intensive Training event. He will share his successful in-depth wealth creation strategies giving delegates a complete toolkit to wealth creation. Approximately 50% of the training sessions focus on property/property related businesses and 50% on other high cash flow start-up business strategies.

Other training packages include pay-as-you go business coaching and a 90-day course of intensive wealth coaching.

To find out more about Kevin and how he can help you please visit
www.kevingreen.co.uk
You can also follow Kevin on Twitter for up to date business news www.twitter.com/kevingreenwales

Coaches and mentors

Some training programs offer follow-up sessions of coaching and mentoring to assist you first hand with your property investments. If this leads to action and you make more money in property deals than you spend on the programme, then it can be worthwhile. Once again, be sure you are going to get the most out of the programme by taking action.

Property sourcers

A key factor in making a profitable investment is finding a below market value property. People sell property for all kinds of reasons. You can find deals through estate agents or at auctions but some deals never appear on the agent's books. A property sourcer is someone who advertises through leaflet drops or newspaper ads, offering to buy properties fast for cash.

If a homeowner is on the verge of repossession, it can be an advantage for them to sell the house before this happens. They can then pay off the mortgage and other debts and move on. They escape the stress of repossession and avoid damaging their credit rating. In this way property can sometimes be sold at 20 or 30% less than its full market value. The sourcer will set up this deal and then sell it on to an investor for a fee. This arrangement can work for all concerned.

Unfortunately, some excesses in this area have led to government legislation banning buy-and-rent-back schemes. Personally, I get uncomfortable when I read of people who hang out at doctors' surgeries and law courts to find distressed homeowners. Ensure that any deal you find in this way is ethically sourced. You need also to be sure that the deal you are buying is genuine. Are the purchase price and rental figures accurate? To check this you will need to do your own research. Again, you have to ask whether you could find just as good a deal yourself.

Property investor networks

Being a landlord can be a lonely game. Where better to meet other landlords and to learn about property investing first-hand than at a property network meeting. In the usual format the evening begins with networking. Then there may be one or two talks by an expert about some aspect of property investment. You always learn something new. Hearing about others' struggles and achievements can both warn and inspire. There is usually an update from a mortgage broker on the latest trends in the lending market. Other news affecting landlords may be shared. An entrance fee is usually charged on the night.

Landlords' associations

You may wish to become a member of a landlords' association. These bodies charge an annual subscription for membership. You will have access to an advice helpline, management software and many other support services. Some offer training courses which are discounted to members.

Property investment companies

There are companies in the UK that will help you invest in property. These can take the form of a property business franchise, or a package of services designed to help you get started. This can be a good route into property investment for people who can raise a deposit but have little inclination for doing it all themselves. There are fees of course, but if discounts are obtained on your properties then your fees are covered. To learn how to do it so well yourself, you could spend a lot more on training courses.

When considering buying property with the assistance of a property company, you should do some due diligence before committing yourself. Find out how long they have been trading and what track record they have. Ask for testimonials from satisfied customers. The Trading Standards Institute, which is a government consumer watchdog, will have records of complaints against any rogue traders. Do your own research on the properties which are offered for investment and ask to view them before purchasing. Choose a company which offers you a professional service, but which doesn't tie you in.

Whichever route you take into property investment, it is good to have a general knowledge of the basic principles. In the next chapter I will walk you through the process of buying and renting out your first investment property.

A one-stop-shop – Midas Property School.

Midas Property School stands out as a unique property investment service. They bring together a team of property professionals to assist the investor in each step of the investment process. The service is tailored to each client's objective and desired outcome. A typical goal is to build a portfolio of ten properties over a ten-year period. Because of this long-term goal, the Midas team remains in touch with investors and offers on-going support.

Sourcing: Properties are sourced in parts of the UK where house prices are rising fastest. Extensive research is carried out on the area of each development to ensure there is high rental demand.

Discounts: A discount of up to 20% can be negotiated with the developer. All discounts are passed on to the investor.

The purchase process: An independent mortgage broker is on hand to help the investor find the best mortgage product for his or her needs. A solicitor works with Midas clients to make the purchase process as smooth as possible.

Letting: The Midas property manager will contact up to forty letting agents who operate in the vicinity of the property. Only those who answer promptly are considered. The best agents are selected and asked to advertise the property. In this way the most efficient agent is engaged. A professional video inventory of the property is commissioned.

Management: Midas also holds the agent accountable on the investor's behalf and keeps them under review. A 24/7/365 maintenance service is arranged to cover all eventual emergency breakdowns. Rent reviews are carried out annually to ensure the rent reflects the current market rate. This provides maximum profitability.

Growing the portfolio: As the properties are in areas of the UK where prices are still rising, equity can be accumulated. Each year a review of the portfolio is carried out to plan the next investment. In this way the investor can build a portfolio over time using just one initial capital investment.

A Buffer. Setting some money aside as a buffer is a key element of the Midas approach. Having a reserve of cash ensures that unforeseen events do not endanger your investments. The insistence on a buffer makes Midas a safer route to property investment.

www.defuseyourpensiontimebomb.com/midas

Telephone: 0117 907 3880

Email: contact@defuseyourpensiontimebomb.co.uk

Chapter Eight

The anatomy of a buy-to-let

There is more than one way to skin a cat, as the saying goes. There are also multiple ways to approach investing in property. We have looked at a sample of the wide variety of services available to assist you. We have also noted that you may have strengths and aptitudes you can put to work. It's up to you to decide how you want to go about it. In this chapter we'll assume that you are going to do it all yourself. Even if you employ professionals for all or some of the tasks, you need to know what to expect so that you can hold them to account.

Cash flow or capital growth?

There are two factors to consider when starting your research: cash flow and capital growth. Cash flow refers to the rental profit you can obtain each month after mortgage payments and fees have been paid. This may be your priority if your short-term aim is to supplement your income. To maximise cash flow you will be looking in an area with low house prices and relatively high rental potential. Ex-local authority housing is usually good for cash flow.

Capital growth means the price of the property will rise higher and faster. If your job provides a good income and your main goal is to build up a pension pot, then you'll be aiming for capital growth. Look for an area where house prices are growing or are set to grow in the near future. You may need to invest in another part of the country to obtain maximum growth potential. In 2011 Midas Property School sourced flats in Stratford, overlooking the Olympic park. The investment that has gone into this part of London will cause property prices to soar.

When we were looking to buy a flat in Bristol, I did several viewings in various parts of the city. Then I made a comparison chart to help me crunch the numbers and analyse the merits of each property. One of the flats was a brand new, luxury apartment near the centre of town. This would have been excellent for capital growth over time. However, it required a large deposit and the service charge was high. So cash flow was not so good. It turned out that an ex-local authority flat I had seen would give me more monthly return and reasonable growth over time. So we bought the less glamorous property.

Do your research

Location, location, location. Choosing a property in the right area is key to success. Good research will help you to narrow in on the area that suits your priorities. You will be looking for an up and coming area, with strong rental demand. Identify areas set to grow in value. Look for stories in the media about population growth. Is there a part of town that is about to benefit from major investment? New factories, new schools and new infrastructure can mean increased demand and rising house prices. Your local council planning officer can inform you of planned investment. You should always buy properties located close to public transport and amenities. Avoid flats above takeaways however, as noise and strong smells can put tenants off.

Choosing the right area

is key to success.

Walk around an area and look for scaffolding and skips. This shows that the residents are improving their properties. Check if the gardens are neat or if they are full of junk. Is there a lot of graffiti, or signs of vandalism? These affect house prices. Check crime figures for the area. What is the quality of the local shops? Thriving commerce shows a thriving community. Chat to people in pubs and at bus stops. Ask what it is like to live around here. Try to get a feel for the area. You may find that Starbucks has very kindly spent thousands of pounds to do your research for you, as their shops are located in up-and-coming areas.

Some recommend that you run a dummy ad in a newspaper for a house to let. Note the details of houses that you are interested in buying. Then place an ad for this house. If you receive few enquiries, then you know this property is not in demand. If the phone is ringing off the hook, then buy it. We tried this when doing research for our first property. I had lots of enquiries, including one from an airline pilot.

If your priority is cash flow, you may be looking at buying an ex-local authority property. These properties are usually cheaper and often achieve similar rents to private properties. Since the right-to-buy scheme of the 1980s, many properties in social housing estates are now owner occupied.

Just be careful not to buy in any part of the estate where anti-social behaviour is a problem.

Research has never been easier than today, thanks to the numerous internet sites dedicated to the property market. There are Rightmove, Hometrack, and Mouseprice, to name a few. Internet research is a good place to start, but nothing replaces feet on the ground. Speak to local letting agents and ask them what types of property are in high demand. Which properties are easiest to let? What level of rent is achievable?

Types of investment property

There are several types of investment property. Houses and flats may be let to individuals or families. An HMO (House of Multiple Occupancy) can be let to students or professionals. Holiday lets in the UK or abroad are also good investments. We will take a closer look at these in chapter ten. But for now we will assume you are going to buy a house or a flat to let with a single AST.

How to search on Rightmove

Open an account on the Rightmove website. Enter the postcode of a given area and click on *properties for sale*. Then choose, *this post code only, house, min bedrooms-2, maximum bedrooms-4, maximum price-£150,000, minimum price-no minimum*. Then sort the results by *lowest price*. Look at the properties which seem to be priced to sell (filter out the shared ownership properties). You can find their location on the map. Take note of the sale price. Save these properties in your account.

Then open Rightmove on a new tab. Type in the same postcode and click on *properties for rent*. Enter *this postcode only*, and the same details as before. Maximum rent £1,000. Scroll through the results until you find houses similar to the ones you have saved in your first search. Try to find the identical house in the same street. Take note of the rental value. You can then use the formula below to work out if the area is suitable for investment.

How to work out the yield.

The gross yield for a property is calculated as follows:

Formula for yield.

$$\frac{R \times 100}{PP} = Y$$

R = annual rent, PP = purchase price. Y = Yield.

I have tried to keep this calculation as simple as possible, but if your eyes glaze over at the sight of formulas, then your best plan will be to find a friend who can help you do the maths. It is important to get this right because you do not want to be losing money every month when you could be earning money. There are many people who buy investment property that costs them money. You can avoid this.

You need to find a property with a gross yield of at least 8%.

How to conduct a viewing

When you have identified several potential investment properties, you can request the details from the agent. If you do this on Rightmove, the agent will call you to get your details and to arrange a viewing. At this point you can begin to establish a rapport with the agent. Tell them the kind of property you are looking for. They may have other similar properties for sale. Ask to be put on their list of contacts. Remember that the agent will not necessarily know which properties work best for investment. That is for you to work out.

One of the first questions the agent will ask you is, "How much do you want to spend on a property purchase?" The best answer is, "As little as possible." If you reveal too much about your financial position, the agent will use this information to advise the vendor that you are able to pay more. At this point just inform the agent that you have a deposit in place and that your mortgage broker has qualified you in principle for a buy-to-let mortgage.

Don't forget that the estate agent is working for the vendor. On the other hand, the agent's goal is to sell properties. They only get paid when the sale goes through. For this reason they may drop hints indicating how much the vendor may accept for the property. Listen out for these.

During the viewing take notes on the condition of the property. After three or more houses you will forget what the first one looked like. Record as many details as possible. Check the roof and double-glazing. Ask to see the central heating working. Has any rewiring been done? Are the kitchen and bathroom(s) serviceable, or will they need replacing? Avoid the common mistake of allowing your personal preferences to guide your decision. Remember you will not be living in the property yourself. On a second visit, ask a tradesperson to accompany you. Have him draw up a broad estimate for the works required to prepare the property for letting.

The property business is a people business. As you are walking around the house or flat, talk to the agent about the owner. A simple question is, "What is the vendor's situation?" You are looking for a situation where he or she is able to accept a reduced price for the property.

The property business

is a people business.

You should do as many viewings as possible. The agents will not mind. In fact they will want to show you all the relevant properties on their books. While searching on the internet, it is not always possible to assess a property properly. You may think in advance that some are not suitable, but you never know until you go and see. You can sometimes be surprised. Not all details are recorded on the website. Each time you view a property you are building up a broader base of knowledge that will ultimately help you to discern when a bargain becomes available.

After several viewings, it is a good idea to sit down and do some number crunching. Make a table and enter all the details for each property. Sometimes an apparently good buy can be spoiled by another factor such as a high service charge or high refurbishment costs. Remember this is business, and the bottom line is how much profit will be made each month. When you have identified the best properties it is time to begin putting your offers in.

A basic formula for cash flow

Remember the golden rule in property investing: a good investment will put money in your pocket every month, not take money out. So the interest on the deposit and the mortgage must be less than the rent. (I will assume that your deposit comes from extra borrowing on your home mortgage and that the interest rate for both this and the buy-to-let mortgage is the same).

Here is a basic formula for working out the cash flow of an investment:

Formula for cash flow.

R–(M + C) = CF

R= Rent, M = mortgage, C= costs, CF = Cash Flow

(costs: agent's fees, insurance, repairs, etc.)

When calculating the projected cash flow of a property, remember to factor in all the costs that will be incurred in the running of the investment. If you use an agent, their fees can be between 8 and 15% of the rent, plus VAT. You need to pay for landlord insurance and make an allowance for repairs, maintenance and voids. If you are buying a flat, don't forget the service charge for upkeep of the communal areas. This figure can make a serious dent in your cash flow. Find out in advance what the service charge will be, so you don't get a nasty shock.

How to negotiate

You may be used to the idea that things cost what they are priced at. I once read an article about a jeweller who was having difficulty selling some necklaces. To clear the stock he left instructions for the price to be reduced by 50% and then went on holiday for a week. When he returned he was pleased to find that all the necklaces had been sold. Upon enquiry however, he discovered that the shop assistant had misunderstood his instructions and had increased the prices by 50%! There is value and there is perceived value.

As we've seen, houses are for sale on the property market and it is the market which determines their value. If you have calculated what the house price has to be in order for the deal to work for you, then that is its value to you. If you can satisfy the criteria, then the vendor will sell at the price you offer. Perhaps you will get it cheaper because you are willing to do the necessary work while others want a fully refurbished property. Or because you have finance ready, no chain and can complete the sale within a given time frame. The discount may be negotiated for you by a property professional. Either way, remember that you make a profit when you buy not when you sell.

So let's take an example. We found a property that would have had a usual market value of £120,000. The property was in need of some refurbishment. The owner was deceased and a family member who already has his own home was selling the property. We deduced from this that he may not need every penny he could wring from the sale. Then there were other factors we identified, such as repairs to the central heating and the need for rewiring. Due to its run-down condition the house had been put on the market for £99,950. We decided that the maximum we wanted to pay was £90,000. What should be our first offer? Bear in mind that in a buyer's market most properties sell for around 90% of the asking price, so we thought this was achievable.

A property is only worth what someone is prepared to pay for it.

The first offer should be judged to show the vendor that you are serious and also to display that you expect to pay a lot less than the asking price. We called the agent and made a firm offer of £86,000. We fully expected this offer to be rejected. In fact, if it had not been we would have been disappointed because we could have offered less. At this point the agent came back to us saying something like, "Well Mr. Doherty, the vendor cannot accept your offer but he would accept £96,000." We had just reduced the price.

Now we had to consider our second offer. The increase in your offer will give the vendor the measure of your interest and how much more you are likely to pay. Bear in mind that the third and final offer had to be £90,000, so the second offer had to be £88,000. As we expected, this offer was also rejected. But a counter offer was made. The price had come down significantly and we were making good progress.

So now we made our final offer while at the same time reminding the agent that 90% of the asking price is normal in a buyer's market, that we were ready to proceed immediately, that buyers were thin on the ground and that the property needed a lot of work. We offered £90,000 then told the agent that we had some more viewings to do that afternoon and we might have found a more suitable property. You have to be willing to walk away. This is perfectly normal. The greatest mistake in property investment is to get too attached to a property. This is why property prices rise, because someone "must have that house" and is willing to outbid all others to get it. We waited with baited breath. Then the phone rang, "Congratulations Mr. Doherty, your offer has been accepted." We had just bought ourselves a house!

The purchase process

As soon as your offer is accepted instruct your solicitor to proceed. Give their details to the estate agent. As you already have an agreement in principle with your mortgage broker, you will now ask them to find you the best mortgage deal. Mortgage products can change from day to day, so it is a question of scanning the market and seeing which deal suits you best. For a mortgage to be offered, the lender will require the rent of the property to be at least 1.25 times the monthly mortgage payment.

Formula for mortgage affordability.

I x 1.25 = R

I= monthly interest, R= monthly rent.

You may wonder whether to take a repayment mortgage or an interest-only mortgage. In most cases it will be advisable to have an interest-only mortgage. Interest-only means lower monthly payments and increased cash flow. Much fewer deals will work if you take a repayment mortgage, so you will only be able to buy very cheap property, which may not appreciate so well in value. It will also slow you down in building your portfolio.

However, if you prefer to pay down the mortgage debt from the beginning, it does mean you will have a mortgage free, income-producing property in fifteen or twenty years' time. This can work as long as you can afford the payments in the short term.

Ensure your solicitor is keeping you up-to-date with the progress of the purchase. Ask if every party is in good communication and try to identify who is dragging their feet. It is not unknown for a vendor to pull out of a sale. This can happen for various reasons. Perhaps their circumstances change. Or they just change their mind. Ask the estate agent to tell you of any changes immediately. You can lose money on valuation fees and solicitor's fees if the vendor withdraws the property from the market. In Scotland this is not the case as both parties are legally bound to proceed once the offer is accepted.

Refurbishing your property

Unless you have bought a new property, you will probably have to carry out some work to prepare the house or flat for rental. During the buying process, which can take up to three months, you should ask the vendor for permission to access the property and make a detailed report on the work required. You may have already had an estimate from a builder before buying. Now you can obtain a more detailed quote. If you are planning to do all, or some, of the work yourself, make a list of materials. You can then begin to shop around and look for the best prices. Avoid buying materials at this stage, as you don't want to be left with a lot of materials if the sale falls through.

Decorate the house using neutral colours. Remember it is not for you, but for your tenant. Attractive, but solid kitchen furniture is best. Carpets are cheaper than laminate flooring, but may need replacing more often. Both are acceptable and your budget will guide the decision.

It is your obligation as a landlord to provide heating and a cooker. Other white goods, such as fridge, freezer or washing machine, are optional. Wait and see if your new tenants have their own white goods before buying.

Safety certificates

All rental properties must have a valid gas safety certificate. This can be obtained from a gas engineer. Consider fitting a carbon monoxide alarm near the boiler also.

You will also need an Energy Performance Certificate (EPC). In the future rental properties may be taxed according to their energy rating. Upgrading the boiler and laying loft insulation will improve this rating. Check if grants are available for this work.

Smoke detectors are strongly recommended in all rental properties. Hard-wired, linked detectors are preferred, but battery detectors are acceptable. Tenants can sometimes remove a detector that goes off when the toast is burned. You can fit a heat detector near the kitchen to prevent this. Your local fire authority may offer free fire safety checks. Consider fitting a fire safety blanket in the kitchen.

Landlords are responsible for the safety of the electrical installation in their property. The 17th edition of the IEE wiring regulations came into force in 2008. If the house was wired before this it may need some updating. The Electrical Safety Council (ESC) recommends that a periodic inspection and test is carried out by a registered electrician at intervals not exceeding five years, or on a change of tenancy. The electrician will issue an Electrical Installation Condition Report (EICR) which details any damage, deterioration, or defects within the installation. When a new consumer unit is installed you will receive an Electrical Installation Certificate. This serves the same purpose as the EICR.

Finding a tenant

Your research will have shown that your property is in demand. You need to decide in advance whether you are going to advertise and rent out the property yourself, or use the services of a letting agent. As we've already mentioned, we've had mixed experiences with letting agents. Just as the agent has to check out the tenant, you need to check out the agent before asking them to let your property.

The agent should carry out a credit reference check. This will reveal whether or not the tenant owes money or has a poor credit rating. An agent once found that one of our prospective tenants had a CCJ (County Court Judgment). He claimed he didn't know that he had one. We preferred not to rent the property to him.

The letting agent will use a specialist credit referencing agency to carry out these checks. Many of these agencies also offer a rent guarantee. If the agency is confident the person is credit-worthy, they will guarantee the rent, for a fee. It works like an insurance policy. What most people do not know is that you can also use this credit referencing service yourself without passing through a letting agent.

When your property is advertised you may be asked whether you accept tenants who receive housing benefit. Housing benefit is paid directly into your bank account, so in a way it is more certain as long as the tenants' circumstances do not change. Many people would consider that a wealthier tenant in a better area would always make a better tenant than a lower income person in a poorer area. But I have known people to be disappointed in tenants in any kind of area. As we've seen, to be a landlord you do need a basic belief in human nature. There are good people and not so good people in all walks of life, so keep an open mind. Contact the housing team at your local council for more information.

The basic legal document establishing the rights of landlord and tenant is the Assured Shorthold Tenancy agreement. This can be set up for six or twelve months, or any period that you agree with your tenant. You may wish to avoid the agreement running out in December or January, as these are months when fewer people want to move. So, for example, a contract signed in June would be for eight months instead of six.

You must also receive a deposit from the tenant, usually equivalent to one month's rent. The purpose of the deposit is to pay for the repair of any damage to the property. It must be deposited by the landlord in an independently monitored scheme, such as the Deposit Protection Scheme (DPS). The agent will arrange this for you if your property is fully managed.

> To be a landlord you need a basic
>
> belief in human nature.

You also need to do an inventory of the fixtures and fittings and the state of repair at the beginning of the tenancy. The tenant and the landlord must sign the inventory. It has to be dated on the first day of the tenancy; otherwise it cannot be used to prove the condition of the property in case of disputes at the end of the tenancy. Increasingly, photographic or video inventories are used.

Managing your property

Property investment is a business that, once set up, requires only occasional intervention. If you buy a new property your repair and maintenance issues should be kept to a minimum. If you invest in an older property make sure you have it refurbished to a good standard. Of course you will still get calls for repairs, and chances are that the call to tell you about a broken water drainage pipe will not come on a Monday morning. It will come on a Sunday morning, preferably Easter Sunday or better still Christmas day! From the outset you need to decide whether you want to take the calls yourself or have your property managed so that someone else will take them.

If you live far away, or you do not want to take care of maintenance and repairs yourself, then have your property fully managed. If you want to grow your portfolio beyond a few properties this is the preferred option. Many landlords prefer to save money by managing the property themselves. However, after two or three properties the work becomes too much and they stop buying. So doing everything yourself can be a false economy in the long run.

Another option is to employ your own property manager. If you are in business, you could train one of your administrative staff to look after the paperwork and arrange repairs to your properties.

The emergency call may come on Christmas day!

When your property is fully managed the agent will deal with all repairs. They will decide with you on a maximum amount, say £100, to be spent on a repair job without your express permission. Larger jobs will need your approval before proceeding. It is important to remember though, that at all times you, the owner, remain responsible for the condition of the property. I know landlords who allow their properties to get run down, or who put off repairs to essential things for too long. This makes no sense, as a tenant who is discontent will leave at the first opportunity. Voids can be expensive. The property is your asset, so it is in your interest to keep it in a good condition. A good letting agent will carry out inspections every three to six months. This will alert you to maintenance problems and ensure the tenants are looking after the property. You must give the tenant twenty-four hours' notice before carrying out an inspection.

Case study – Jenny

Investing at a distance

We have been investing in property since 2009 as a strategy for retirement.

My husband and I live and work in Kenya and our income is made up of voluntary gifts from friends and supporters. Over the years we have not been able to build up a sufficient pension to give us a realistic income for our later years.

We were due to inherit some money from our parents and we had the idea of investing in property. We were inspired by John's enthusiasm and encouragement.

On a visit to the UK for a few months we started looking for property in Bristol. We didn't really know what kind of property to look for. It was all very daunting. I do not think it would ever have happened but for our friend John's advice. We gained confidence from his back up. We eventually found two flats and it was obvious that they were a good deal.

We had returned to Kenya by the time the flats completed in May 2009. We asked John to prepare the flats for letting. We signed up an agent to manage them in our absence. Before long we had them rented out. The additional income has been very welcome.

Although we bought newly refurbished flats, there were some issues with repairs and maintenance. Living abroad, we were unable to see to these ourselves. John has helped us through his company Whitestone Property Services. They have dealt with everything from smelly drains to rats under the floor!

As we prepare to return to the UK we are pleased to know that our retirement income will be a lot more adequate than we could have expected. We've found that property is a sure way to secure the future.

Before the end of the six- or twelve-month period covered by your AST, you need to find out if your tenants wish to stay in the property. You also need to decide if you want them to stay. Carry out an inspection of the property about three months into the tenancy. If you wish to end the agreement after the set period, you need to give the tenant two month's notice in writing. If they wish to leave they must give you one month's notice. When a tenant is staying, you can either set up a new AST for another period or allow the AST to become a Statutory Periodic Tenancy (SPT). The SPT will have the same terms and conditions as the original AST. This is a good time to carry out some upgrades to the property and to review the rent in line with market rates. A fair increase in rent is reasonable and will be accepted by most tenants, especially if they are happy with their home and your good record on repairs and maintenance.

So you're now a property investor. What next? Do you imitate the elephant who wanted to get down from a tree? What did he do? He sat on a leaf and waited for autumn! Should you also just sit back and wait for your retirement? You can do, or you can continue to build your portfolio.

In the next chapter we'll look at how to begin planning ahead. We'll show you how to recover your deposit and use it for your next acquisition. We'll also provide an introduction to exit strategies. But first, let's take a look at some of the most common problems faced by investors and how to deal with them.

Chapter Nine

Planning ahead

Now that you've taken your first step in property investing it's time to begin planning for the future. In this chapter we'll help you consider your next steps and beyond. We'll see how to minimise potential problems and work towards building and protecting a successful property portfolio.

What could possibly go wrong?

If you've ever been around landlords you will doubtless have heard a few nightmare stories. Don't worry; you'll have your own story to tell soon enough! Just remember that your friends are still here to tell the tale, so it isn't that bad. Once again, the right information is crucial to dealing with issues as they arise. The majority of problems fall into one of two categories:

- Tenant problems.

- Cash flow problems.

Buy-to-fret

Your investment property can become a source of stress if tenant problems are not dealt with promptly or, better still, prevented. Non-payment of rent can be a real problem, as you still need to meet mortgage costs. Other tenant issues include damage to property and conflicts with neighbours.

Prevention is better than cure.

As in most things, prevention is better than cure. Taking care to carry out proper checks on candidates for tenancy will filter out potential problems. As we have seen, some credit referencing agencies offer a rent guarantee for tenants who meet the criteria. The tenancy deposit is there to compensate for damage.

In the case of tenants who do not pay the rent and who will not vacate the property, you may need to begin eviction proceedings. Make every effort to resolve the issues with the tenant before this becomes necessary. Keep a record of correspondence and dialogue with the tenant. The process of eviction can take up to six months and can be costly. However, you will have your property returned to you sooner or later. If it comes to this and you cannot face the hassle, consider employing a company to take care of everything for you.

We have had our share of tenant problems. However, you have to realise that every problem has a solution. My advice is to stay calm and work through the difficulties as they arise. Good communication and good will are more than half the battle.

Cash flow problems

Every landlord dreads running out of money. There are several factors which can have a negative impact on cash flow. If you fail to do your research and to correctly analyse the deal, the property can require a monthly top up. Properties which are more difficult to let can have void periods between tenants. We've heard of some property investors who overstretched themselves and were overwhelmed by the mortgage payments. As a result, some have even lost their entire portfolio. Careful planning and good management will prevent this.

Case study – Phil

Working through tenant problems

We were married in 1976 and bought our first house for about £9,000. After six years we moved, selling that house for almost £25,000. Our second house cost £37,500 and sold twenty-one years later for £387,500. Our first investment property was bought in collaboration with a local University to provide accommodation for students.

The benefit of working with the University was that they knew what to expect and were quite helpful, they supplied vetted students and paid the rent directly to us. However, this arrangement came to an abrupt end five years later. The University moved all the students to alternative accommodation after one of our tenants was mugged in the street. We had to find tenants from other sources so I advertised on the internet. I actually found tenants quite easily.

The experience did not put us off, however, and we bought more houses when we downsized. They have been let for several years to married couples and families. We have found most tenants to be decent people. They are happy to pay the rent for a home that they can live in knowing that when the washing machine or central heating packs up the landlord will get it fixed. We have interest-only mortgages and plan to sell some properties to pay off the rest when we retire.

We have had some unfortunate experiences. One family passed the tenancy checks and appeared to be reliable. However, after about two years it became obvious that something was wrong. Rent was being paid erratically and some months not at all. We found it difficult to discuss the situation with the tenant. The man had lost his job and was not easy to approach. Eventually I got help via the advice line of the National Landlords Association. They said I was a very nice person but a poor businessman! I followed their advice and delivered a Notice for Repossession. The tenants left the property owing four months' rent. The property was also in a poor state and needed redecorating throughout. We could have employed a firm to chase them for the money but we have not done this.

Shortly after this experience the main breadwinner in another of our properties was made redundant. The rent began to be paid in smaller amounts and infrequently. The tenant managed to find another job, but it was only temporary. My wife and I decided not to treat the tenant as we had on the previous occasion. Instead, we kept in touch with the breadwinner and developed a spreadsheet to monitor the rent received. I am pleased to say that after seven years this tenant has managed to turn their situation around, they have repaid all the debt and are seriously hoping to purchase the property from us.

Unexpected repair bills can also break the budget. This is where good budgeting will protect you. Carry out a full refurbishment on your property from the start and do regular inspections to keep on top of potential maintenance issues. Find a tradesperson who offers a call out service and agree prices in advance. You can also take out boiler and plumbing insurance.

Another worry for landlords is high interest rates. In 2012 interest rates are at an all-time low. They may remain so for some time given the weak economic recovery. However, they can only go one way from here, up. It is unlikely that we will see the record highs of the early nineties, but rates could return to around 5% above base rate. When you are planning an investment, run a calculation to see what would happen if the interest rates were to rise. If you build in a good margin of profit, your investment will be insulated against the effects of interest rate rises. When interest rates are low it's best to take a mortgage with a fixed rate.

When preparing to invest in property it is important to set aside a reserve of cash to act as a buffer against potential problems. This can be cash in the bank, or it could be in the form of a draw down on your mortgage account. You can arrange this in advance with the lender. A good rule of thumb is to only use two thirds of your available cash at any given time. Although I pass this principle on to you, I must confess I have not always adhered to it myself. We have been close to running out of money at times and the stress involved is not comfortable to bear. Only you can decide what level of risk you want to undertake. It's always best to stay well within your sensible limits.

Some investors have lost their entire portfolio.

Completing the cycle

In the last chapter we saw how, with diligent research and careful negotiation, you can buy a property below its market value. We've also talked about adding value by refurbishing the property. The next step is to apply for extra borrowing on your mortgage based on its new value. Current rules governing lending in the UK state that you must own a house or flat for six months before you are permitted to do this. Although this is common practice it is not automatic. It's at the discretion of the lender. If you intend to re-mortgage, enquire in advance if the bank or building society will allow it.

When you apply for extra borrowing, the lender will ask for a new survey to be carried out. If the value of the property has risen significantly you can borrow up to 80% of the revised figure. You may be able to release part or even all of your original deposit money. You can then use this as a deposit on your next property. This is how it's done!

When the valuation is booked, ask to be present. Inform the tenant in advance and arrange access. It is very important to do your homework before the valuation. Check the prices of sold properties in the immediate area over the past twelve months. Print out details of comparable properties that sold at a high price and bring these with you on the day. When you meet the surveyor, show him around the property and point out the work that has been done since it was last valued. Show him the other property details, then step back and let him do his job. You cannot dictate the price at which your property will be re-valued. However, you need to draw the surveyor's attention to all the elements that could work in your favour.

Your investment can be practically free!

You should be confident in advance of releasing some of the equity you have created in the house, or you shouldn't even try. Otherwise you will incur valuation fees for nothing. You also need to check that the property will still be in a positive cash flow position after re-mortgaging. You may be pleased to see that your whole deposit is returned to you, making your investment practically free!

Reviewing your portfolio

As time goes by you will need to review your portfolio. When house prices are rising you'll be excited to see the equity accumulating in your properties. You can let it accumulate and watch your nest egg build up. Or when there is enough equity, you can use it as a deposit for another investment. In the boom years it was possible to re-mortgage a property the same day as completion. This enabled savvy investors to build up a large portfolio in a short space of time. However the six-month rule introduced in 2008 has made this process a lot slower.

To check that a property remains profitable, you need to work out the return on investment (ROI). You can use the formula below. An ROI of at least 8% should be expected.

Formula for return on investment.

$$\frac{CF \times 100}{D} = ROI$$

CF = Annual cash flow   D = Deposit.

The cost of everything is constantly rising. It seems wages are often the notable exception. However, a strong rental market places an upward pressure on rents. When your property becomes vacant it's the ideal time to check market rates and raise the rent if this is justified. Equally, you may wish to increase the rent for a tenant who has been in residence for several years. Personally I am very slow to do this in a difficult economic climate. But from a strictly business perspective it makes sense.

In the UK 78% of landlords own just one investment property. Only 3% own more than four. Just 8% are full time landlords. Why is this so? Perhaps some do not know how to recycle their deposit and continue investing. Others may be put off by tenant problems. If you decide to grow your portfolio, you can multiply the returns property ownership can offer. When your portfolio reaches its planned size you can then allow the equity to build up. Then you will need to decide how to use this equity in retirement.

Buy and hold versus buy and sell

How long should you keep your investment properties? You will receive different answers to this question depending on who you listen to. Let's look at some of the options. You can decide which one suits you best.

Buy and never sell

Many property experts advocate building a portfolio of properties and holding them indefinitely. There is no doubt that the maximum profit from property is gained over the long term. In addition to rising equity, the profit generated by the rental income will increase over time. If you never sell your properties you can avoid capital gains tax, as you will never realise the profits. However you need to think about inheritance tax. Speak to an Independent Financial Advisor (IFA) about succession planning.

You can access the cash in your portfolio by re-mortgaging. This money is tax free, as it is effectively a loan. You can use it to pay down the mortgage on your home or to buy an annuity guaranteeing an income for the rest of your life. You might even book a cruise to celebrate and reward yourself for your diligence and patience.

The greatest profit from property comes over time.

Buy and sell all on retirement

Another approach is to build a portfolio and wait until a significant capital sum has accumulated before selling and taking all the money out. There are several dangers attached to this strategy. Firstly, you will pay capital gains tax on the profits that the properties have realised. To mitigate this, consider selling your properties over a period of several years in order to make full use of your capital gains tax allowance. Next, remember that once you have bought an annuity your money may be gone forever, as the income produced by most annuities ceases on your death. This approach may suit those want to enjoy the profits of their investments to the full.

Hold some and sell some

This combines the benefits of the other approaches. You can maximise the earning potential of your portfolio by selling some of your least profitable properties. The profits could then be used to reinvest in other deals or to pay off your own mortgage. In a slow rising market your money may stagnate while tied up in equity. This policy will help you to maximise profits. Stagger the sales to make full use of your capital gains tax allowance. As a guide, buy three and sell one.

In this way you can make short-term profits, while building a solid portfolio of income producing properties for the long term. Remember that the greatest profit from property comes over time.

Another benefit of this strategy is that paying off mortgages may improve your credit rating. Lenders like to see loans being paid off. You could find that you have access to mortgages with better conditions as a result.

Taxes relating to property

You probably feel a headache coming on just by thinking about tax. The best advice I can give you is to find a good accountant or an IFA who is well versed in property related tax issues. Here is just a brief guide.

Capital gains tax (CGT)

Capital gains tax is payable on profits realised from the sale of assets. If you make a profit of £30,000 by buying and selling a property you will be taxed on this sum. Fortunately a tax-free allowance is applied to your profit (£10,600 in 2012). The allowance is given to each person who has a share in the profit. So if you buy the property jointly with a partner the capital gains tax allowance applies to each person. In this example you would be taxed on just £8,800. The remaining profit is added to your other income and taxed at your normal rate of income tax.

Be sure to retain all receipts relating to the purchase of your property. It is a good idea to buy an accordion file from a stationer's and to label each section according to the type of expense. In this way you will keep all your receipts safe. Deductible expenses include deposit, solicitor's fees, valuation fees and mortgage setup fees. If you sell the property several years after purchase, the capital gains tax can be very significant. You need to bear this in mind when planning ahead.

Income tax

The profit from the rent of your properties is added to your other income and is subject to income tax. You can deduct all expenses which are "wholly and exclusively" incurred in the running of your buy-to-let business. These include letting agent's fees, accountant's fees, insurance premiums, maintenance and repairs.

Inheritance tax

The threshold for inheritance tax was £325,000 in 2012. This means you will only pay tax on amounts over this threshold. The rate of tax however, is an onerous 40%. When you have added several properties to your portfolio it can easily have a total value of over half a million pounds. Should house prices double in ten years, as they have done historically, then your heirs could face a huge inheritance tax bill when you die. Careful planning can reduce this bill significantly. It is best to seek the advice of an IFA and draw up a plan to avoid a hefty tax bill.

The HMRC website contains lots of information on all aspects of tax. Under "Inheritance Tax" you will find the following citation; "Any gifts you make to individuals will be exempt from Inheritance Tax as long as you live for seven years after making the gift." The story goes that the Queen Mother left it rather late to give away her fortune to her heirs. When in her nineties she asked to see a tax consultant and told him, "One wants to avoid paying tax." She made some donations and was fortunate to live until the age of one hundred and one, thus outliving the seven-year rule for inheritance tax! It is better to plan your donations early.

Making a will

Have you made a will? I know someone who used to say that people who make a will usually die shortly afterwards. Needless to say he did not make one. As a result he left a huge headache for his children to sort out after his death. All his money went by default to his wife who was then in a residential home. Consequently it was all swallowed up in paying the home's fees. Take my advice, make a will.

All his money was swallowed up in care home fees.

This is a huge problem facing some older people today when their house has to be sold to pay for their fees in a residential or nursing home. A properly structured will can prevent this. Use a qualified probate solicitor or seek the advice of an approved will making company.

You may also wish to consider putting in place a lasting power of attorney. This must be done in advance and will be used by your designated agent to make decisions on your behalf regarding your estate, should this become necessary.

Passing on your portfolio

As time goes by, you may consider including your children in ownership of your properties. When your family is young it is hard to imagine them grown up. However, the baby on your knee could one day be your portfolio manager. When your children reach eighteen, you can include them as joint owners of your property. In this way you can greatly reduce your inheritance tax liability. You can also train them to see property as a route to long-term wealth.

As you can see, there are many factors to consider in the long term. Remember that property investing is a team sport. You do not have to have all the answers, but you have to know someone who does. By building a team of professionals you can ensure a profitable and stable investment programme to stand the test of time.

Chapter Ten

Other ways to invest in property

In chapter eight we took a more detailed look at investing in a single residential property, such as a house or flat. There are many other ways to invest in property. Books and websites providing specialist advice are available. In this chapter I will take you on a whistle-stop tour of some of the forms and vehicles which are open to you.

Investing in property through your pension

Saving for a pension used to be very limited and inflexible. You could only put your money into a fund that was invested for you by a pension provider. However, in recent years the government has allowed greater individual freedom to invest in a wide range of options.

One of these is a Self-Invested Personal Pension (SIPP). SIPPs can be used to invest your money in a variety of funds, according to your choice. They can now also be used to invest in property. This is a very exciting development for savers, as there is no tax to pay on either rental profits or capital appreciation. SIPPs are regulated by the Financial Services Authority and the regulations controlling them are updated regularly so you need to seek the advice of an Independent Financial Advisor. Here is just a brief summary.

All rental profits and capital appreciation are tax free.

Commercial Property SIPP. A business owner can transfer business premises into a SIPP. The company will pay rent on the premises, but instead of being lost, the money will contribute to the growth of the pension fund.

Overseas Property SIPP. SIPPs have now been expanded to include certain types of overseas property developments. These are usually holiday resort apartments which are bought off-plan.

Property Funds. Those who do not want to own property can still benefit from the property market. Property funds and land investments can be accessed via a SIPP.

As with all pension contributions, SIPPs qualify for tax relief. In this way the government can help you build a property portfolio. How cool is that? But that is not all. The clever part of a property pension is that the pension fund can also borrow money. This is a very attractive option for those with a substantial pension pot who are disappointed with the growth of their traditional pension.

Holiday lets

Perhaps you like the idea of owning a holiday home by the sea or in the country. With the knowledge you have already gained by reading this book you will know why a savvy investor would never choose a caravan over a holiday chalet. You can find both on a typical holiday park but they are very different. One will lose all its value over time and the other will increase in value over time.

The first thing to point out is that it is more difficult to achieve profitability with holiday lets than with a residential let. As a result this is not a sure route to building up your retirement fund. To make a profit from a holiday home in the UK you need to buy a quality property, refurbish it to a high standard and be very hands-on with the rentals. You can turn a profit, but it's hard work.

We stayed in a lovely chalet with a stunning sea view in North Devon last year. It was beautifully presented and furnished. The owners marketed it through their own website. They called us on the Friday night to check everything was okay. Chalets like this can be bought for as little as £25,000 at the moment, as the market has fallen from its peak in 2007. A nice property in a good location can be expected to rise in value as the economy recovers. Positive cash flow may be difficult to achieve in the short-term, but if your goal is simply to cover some of your costs while enjoying the freedom to use the chalet yourself whenever you can, then it can be a great addition to your property portfolio.

Property abroad

At the height of the property boom many people were investing in property overseas. Spain, Bulgaria and Florida were among the most popular destinations. This bubble has now well and truly burst. The Spanish property market is at an all-time low. However, if you have some spare cash and you do not mind taking a long-term view you can pick up a real bargain. This is a specialist area and you should do extensive research before investing. As always, the right property, in the right location, can bring a substantial return.

Case study – Shaun

Home and away

I was twenty-one when I bought my first house. My mum had a friend who lived nearby who was moving away. So mum suggested I buy the friend's house to have my own home.

Being a builder, I wanted to extend the house. To begin with I built a garage on the side. I later added to the extension and it eventually became a completely separate house. I rented out both houses when I moved to another home.

Sometime later my mum went to Bulgaria to buy a retirement property. I went out with her and had a look at the Bulgarian property market, which was booming at the time. Mum wanted to buy in a quiet village, but we preferred the Black Sea coast. Properties were more expensive in Sunny Beach however and we thought we would not have enough. We went around several estate agents, and one told us of an off plan development which had just come on the market. We put down a deposit and paid the instalments as the apartment block was being built. I used the equity we had created in the new build house to fund these investments. We later bought another apartment in this way.

I have to say I have not really had any problems with property investment. I used an agent to find my first tenant and the properties have been rented out by word of mouth since then. The tenants know that I expect them to look after the property and pay the rent on time. A key element in my success is my partner's administration talents. She is the one who knows all the facts and figures and who keeps the paperwork in order. We make a good team.

On the plus side, we have enjoyed many holidays in our apartment in Bulgaria. We also rent the other apartment to friends and family, so lots of people have enjoyed them.

Our plan is to pay off the mortgages of our properties in fifteen years. This will leave us with pure rental income. We do this by taking only repayment mortgages. As a result, we do not have any income in the short term as the rent just covers the mortgage and costs.

Do not be greedy, is what I would say to someone starting out in property today. Do not be quick to spend your profits, but keep reinvesting. In this way you will build up a good retirement income.

Houses of Multiple Occupancy (HMO)

A house let out to students or professionals on a room with shared kitchen and bathroom basis is called an HMO. They can provide excellent cash flow. HMOs fall into two categories: licensed and unlicensed. For an HMO with up to four tenants a licence is not required. The cash flow from these properties can be high provided all the rooms remain occupied. The down side is the increased management workload to keep the property in full occupancy. Four tenants require four separate contracts. Single people are likely to move more than a family with children at school. Books and training courses are available to help you buy and run an HMO. Check your local council website for details of legislative requirements.

Rent a room

To provide additional income, or to help you save a deposit for your first property investment, you could consider renting out a room in your house. Several websites are now dedicated to this service. Obviously you need to think about the practicalities and your security. Sharing your home will certainly present some restrictions on your privacy. But it can be a very useful source of income. The government offers a generous tax break through the Rent-a-room scheme. You can earn up to £4,250 a year tax-free by letting furnished rooms in your home. Check the government website for details (www.direct.gov.uk)

Rent out a house you inherit

One easy way into property investment is to rent out your parents' or relatives' house when it becomes yours. Where several children are due to inherit you could agree to let it jointly and share the income. The accumulated equity can contribute towards a pension plan for all concerned. Alternatively you may be able to buy your siblings' share. If the house is mortgage-free it can provide good rental income. Or you could use some of the equity as a deposit for a second investment property.

Chapter Eleven

What are you going to do now?

So much more could be said about property investment as a vehicle for building wealth. However I do not want this book to become a tome that no one will ever pick up. Besides, there are many people more qualified than me who have written excellent books on the various aspects of the subject. The purpose of this book is to open your mind and get you thinking.

What have you learned?

In these brief chapters I have tried to make you aware of the worsening prospects for pensioners in the UK. The situation has been described by financial commentators as a ticking time bomb and a future apocalypse. You only have to see the difficulties faced by a number of today's pensioners to realise that things are getting worse, not better.

We have looked at the track record of property as a means of wealth creation and wealth preservation. We have seen how property can be leveraged to multiply the gains of a rising market. We have explained that property is an excellent hedge against the money corroding power of inflation.

Tomorrow never comes.

You now know that property investing is a team sport. You can begin to build a network of professionals and fellow investors to help increase your chances of success. You know how to get started in your research and where to find further instructions.

Procrastination is the thief of time

When are you going to get started? Remember time is seldom found; it has to be made. The reason why most people leave it until it is too late to build up an adequate pension, is they keep telling themselves they will do it later when they have more money. But you will never do anything tomorrow, because tomorrow never comes. The only time zone you can act in is *today*.

During the period when I was looking into property investment and weighing the options, I was also corresponding by email with my mother's cousin in Toronto, Canada. We were working together on building a family tree. I happened to mention I was doing research into property. He wrote back to tell me with a tinge of sadness, that years before he had considered buying a condominium beside one of the lakes north of Toronto. I think they were selling for less than $50,000 CAD at the time. He said these same properties were now worth over a million dollars. I felt sad for him because as a self-employed small business owner he was unable to retire and worked almost until he passed away in 2009. This was one of the things that spurred me on to take the plunge.

Analysis paralysis

We have emphasised the importance of research and training to achieve successful outcomes in property investment. Now we have to tell you that if you attend some property seminars you will meet a lot of people who suffer from *analysis paralysis*. To get anywhere you will have to take action sooner or later.

Jane Austen has one more lesson to teach us. One of her characters, Lady Catherine de Bourgh, had a very high opinion of herself and her abilities. While insisting on being included in a conversation about music, she exclaimed, "There are few people in England, I suppose, who have more true enjoyment of music than myself, or a better natural taste. If I had ever learnt, I should have been a great proficient."

It's always easy to sit on the sidelines and imagine how things should be done. But until you get started you can't really express a valid opinion. Settle in your mind that your investments will not be perfect. Do your best for now and get perfect later. The main objective is to make an investment that will not cost you money every month and will rent out easily. There are many hundreds of thousands of properties in the UK which would make excellent investments. So do not get hung up trying to find the perfect one.

What's your plan?

Do you have an action plan? The plan for some people is the National Lottery. The best definition I have heard of the Lottery is that it is a tax on people who are not good at maths! I am sorry to tell you this and I hope you are not offended. My intentions are good. The Lottery is a complete waste of money. You would be better to put the money in a good savings scheme.

The opportunity is now

Today there is nothing stopping anyone from becoming a landlord. Who can tell what legislation will be passed in the future? It could become more difficult for the average person to become a property investor. Now is the time to take the opportunity.

House prices are lower now than at any time since 2004. Interest rates are low. Mortgage finance is becoming more available. You may struggle to find a better set of circumstances to start your investment career.

Life's too short

In my work as an electrician I often find myself climbing over the contents of someone's loft. One day I was working for a family who had lived in their house for many years. The whole story of the family was laid out before me; the toddler's toys, the Lego, the train set, the old computers. The children had grown up and were making their own way in the world. Life goes by so quickly and it reminds us to focus on what is really important.

Now that you have reached the end of this brief introduction to the world of property investing, you have begun to equip yourself to face its challenges and opportunities. Try to remember how you felt about property investing before you started reading. How do you feel now? Has your increased knowledge begun to dispel your fear? I hope so.

I wish you well in your new role as a landlady or landlord. Be a good one and let me know how you get on. If only one person emails to say they have found the confidence to make their first investment, I will be satisfied.

Annexe 1

How to calculate your personal pension deficit.

Step 1. Find out at what age you will receive state pension.

Info is here: http://en.wikipedia.org/wiki/UK_State_Pension

Step 2. Find out how much you can expect to accumulate in your pension fund by the time you reach retirement age.

Include state pension and all private pensions.

Ask for a pension forecast from the DWP: http://www.direct.gov.uk/en/pensionsandretirementplanning/statepensio n/statepensionforecast/dg_10014008

Ask your private pension provider for a forecast.

If you have several pensions, contact your former employers to gather details. Find out how much each pension can be expected to produce in terms of retirement income.

Step 3. Calculate how much income you can expect to receive when you retire.

Use an online annuity calculator to forecast your retirement income.

http://www.find.co.uk/pensions/annuities_centre/annuities-calculator

Add to this any passive income you can expect to receive such as dividends from stocks and shares, royalties or income from property.

Step 4. Make an estimation of your living costs on retirement.

Draw up a detailed budget of your financial needs on retirement. The spreadsheet below can help you. Remember your mortgage may be paid off by the time you retire. You can also deduct child expenses. On the other hand you may want to have some extra money to treat yourself or your grandchildren. As a general guide you can expect to need at least 2/3rds of your current income.

There are several online guides on the websites of pension providers. Below is an example.

http://www.standardlife.co.uk/1/site/uk/pensions/getting-started/income

Step 5. Work out your personal pension deficit.

By deducting your projected retirement income from your estimated expenses you will have a broad idea of your financial position on retirement. Remember that income from most annuities does not increase over time. The cost of living, on the other hand, continues to rise.

The shortfall may be alarming. Better to find out now than the day you retire. It could give you the motivation you need to do something about it.

Step 6. Work out how much extra you will need to save towards your retirement.

You basically have two options. Either save more in a traditional pension, or invest in income producing assets such as property. Use a pension pot calculator to work out how much you will need to save each month to make up the shortfall on retirement. You can search for a calculator online or click on this link.
http://www.thisismoney.co.uk/money/pensions/article-1633402/Pension-pot-calculator-How-need-save-retirement.html

At this point you will need to speak to your financial advisor about a new pension plan.

There are several websites which can help you.

http://www.pensionsadvisoryservice.org.uk/

http://www.direct.gov.uk/en/Pensionsandretirementplanning/PlanningForRetirement/DG_10014582

http://www.ageuk.org.uk/money-matters/pensions/

http://www.thisismoney.co.uk/money/pensions/index.html

Retirement budget spread sheet.

Food	
Household goods	
Clothes	

Car renewal	
Car servicing/repairs	
Road tax	
Car insurance	
Fuel	
Income tax	
Pharmacy	
Dental fees	
House insurance	
House repairs	
Council tax	
Water	
Electricity/gas	
Furniture/appliances	
Mobile phone	
Telephone	
TV licence	
TV/internet	
Leisure/gym	
Pets	
Travel	
Holidays	
Credit cards/loans	

Accountant/legal fees	
Bank fees	
Giving	
Books	
Newspapers/magazines	
Family gifts	
Stamps/stationary	
Medical costs	
Dining out	
Miscellaneous	

Annexe 2

Annuity rates graph

Over the last decade or so the annuity rates offered at retirement have reduced significantly.

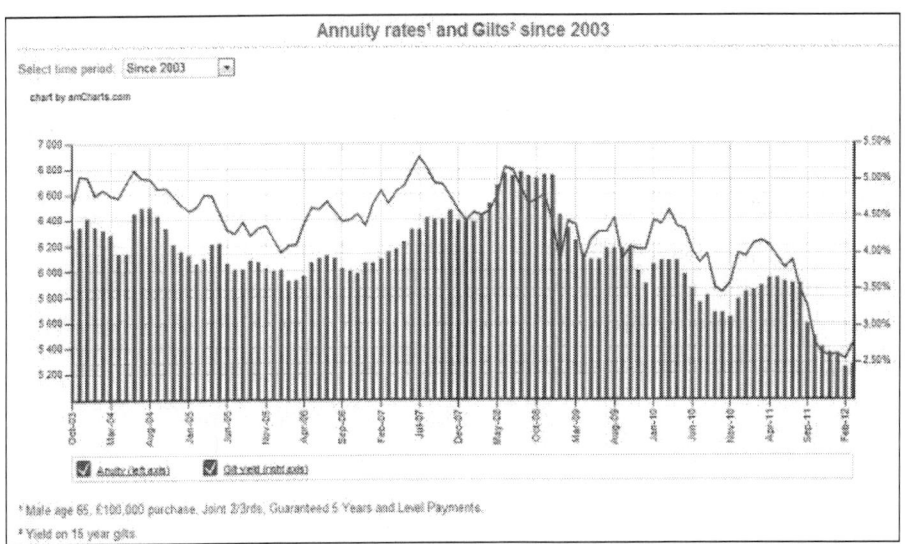

Source : http://www.thisismoney.co.uk/money/pensions/article-2144723/UK-pension-income-battered-eurozone-crisis-annuity-rates-face-fresh-falls.html

Annexe 3

Annuity tables for standard annuity rates, 2011 (sample)

Annual income.

Male lives Pension fund	Age 60	Age 65	Age 70	Age 74
£35,000	£2172	£2436	£2724	£3132
£50,000	£3108	£3432	£3912	£4500
£75,000	£4680	£5184	£5880	£6756

Female lives Pension fund	Age 60	Age 65	Age 70	Age 74
£35,000	£2004	£2232	£2544	£2880
£50,000	£2892	£3204	£3648	£4140
£75,000	£4344	£4824	£5496	£6228

Joint life, with 50% spouse's pension benefit Pension fund	Male age 65, Female age 63	Male age 70, Female age 68
£35,000	£2184	£2412
£50,000	£3084	£3456
£75,000	£4644	£5208

Source : http://www.rightannuity.co.uk/2011/annuity-tables-for-standard-annuity-rates/

Annexe 4

Formulae for property investing

Formula for yield.

$$\frac{R \times 100}{PP} = Y$$

R = annual rent, PP = purchase price. Y = Yield.

Formula for cash flow.

$$R-(M + C) = CF$$

R= Rent, M = mortgage, C= costs, CF = Cash Flow

(costs: agent's fees, insurance, repairs, etc.)

Formula for mortgage affordability.

$$I \times 1.25 = R$$

I= monthly interest, R= monthly rent.

Formula for return on investment.

$$\frac{CF \times 100}{D} = ROI$$

CF = Annual cash flow   D = Deposit.

Annexe 5

Websites for property research

www.rightmove.co.uk

www.zoopla.co.uk

www.nethouseprice.co.uk

www.hometrack.co.uk

www.checkmyarea.com

www.mouseprice.co.uk

www.upmystreet.com

Further Reading

David Lawrenson, *Successful Property Letting*, 2011.

Tony Booth, *The Buy to Let Manual*, 2007.

Neil Mansell, *Wage Slave to Financial Freedom*, 2011.

Howard Goodie, *Buying Bargains at Property Auctions*, 2005.

Rupert Hunt and Matthew Hutchinson, *The Essential Guide to Flat Sharing*, 2009.

Robert Kiyosaki, *Rich Dad, Poor Dad*, 2011.

Susan Jeffers, *Feel the Fear and Do It Anyway*, 1987.

Jeff Olson, *The Slight Edge*, 2005.

Property Glossary

Accountant: can help fill in your self-assessment tax return and advise on tax issues.

Annuity: is purchased with pension funds to provide an income for life.

Analysis paralysis: state of inertia caused by over emphasis on research.

AST: the Assured Shorthold Tenancy agreement is the basic legal document which sets out the duties and responsibilities of landlord and tenant.

Auction: the highest bidder can sometimes buy property quickly and cheaply.

Buy-to-let: purchase of a house or flat to rent out to a tenant.

Capital gains tax: tax incurred on the sale of assets.

Cash flow: monthly profit from rental properties.

Coach: experienced investor who gives investment advice according to your personal circumstances.

Credit referencing: checks carried out on the credit record of a potential tenant.

Deposit: amount paid up front by the tenant (usually equivalent to one month's rent) as a guarantee against damage to the property.

Electrical safety certificate: an Electrical Installation Condition Report must be carried out by a registered electrician. Valid for five years.

EPC: Energy Performance Certificate. Official record of the energy efficiency of the property. Valid for ten years.

Estate agent: represents the vendor in the sale of a property.

Fear of failure: common fear which prevents many people from starting a new enterprise.

Gas Safety: certificate issued by a registered engineer which attests the safety of a domestic gas installation. Valid for twelve months.

HMO: house of multiple occupancy. Building shared by individuals who are not related.

Holiday let: apartment, chalet, house or cottage which is rented out to holidaymakers for a short period.

Housing benefit: social security payment for rent.

Inheritance tax: tax incurred on a deceased estate.

Income tax: tax incurred on rental profits.

Inspections: checks carried out to assess the need for repairs and maintenance to a property.

Insurance: landlord's insurance covers the building and fixed contents.

Inventory: detailed record of the condition of a property on the day the tenant moves in.

Investment: sum of money paid out in the hope of a greater return.

Joint venture: two or more people pool funds, knowledge and skills to make an investment.

Landlord: owner of a rental property.

Landlord association: provides information and assistance to members.

Legacy: that which remains after death.

Letting agent: advertises a property for rent and vets potential tenants. Can also manage rental property.

Meet: gathering of property investors.

Mentor: offers personal guidance for investment decisions.

Mind-set: way of thinking.

Mortgage broker: independent agent who searches the whole of the market to find the best mortgage product.

Mortgage offer: letter confirming a mortgage has been granted and setting out the terms and conditions.

Negotiation: exchange between buyer and vendor to establish a mutually agreed sale price.

Network: gathering of property investors.

Offer: amount of money proposed by the vendor.

Overseas property: holiday rental properties outside the UK.

Pension deficit: the shortfall of money between expenses and income on retirement.

Pension pot: total amount saved in a pension fund.

Private pension: optional saving plan for retirement.

Procrastination: putting decision off indefinitely.

Property development: buying or building a property with a view to selling it at a profit.

Property investment: buying a property which will increase in value over time.

Property management: caring for rented properties and their tenants.

Public sector pension: savings fund provided for government employees.

ROI: return on investment. The annual rental profit expressed as a percentage of the deposit.

Self-Assessment: tax return which must be completed by sole traders.

Seminars: events where property investment is taught.

Service charge: fee covering the expenses of the communal areas and exteriors of flats and apartment buildings.

SIPP: Self invested personal pension. Funds in a SIPP may be used to invest in property.

Smoke alarms: alarms to detect signs of fire. Required in HMO's. Strongly recommended in all rental properties.

Sourcers: people who arrange property deals.

Statutory Periodic Tenancy: tenancy agreement which succeeds AST by default.

State pension: compulsory government retirement savings scheme.

Tax planning: property investment strategy to minimise tax liabilities.

Training: non-academic teaching on property investment.

Viewing: visit and inspection of a property for sale.

Will: official record of intentions regarding the property of a deceased estate.

Yield: gross annual percentage profit on a rental property.

Index

End Notes

[i] Malcolm McClean, *State pension age: what the latest changes mean*. BBC business website, 19th Oct 2011. (http://www.bbc.co.uk)

[ii] Bis

[iii] Dan Hyde, Year of the pensions crunch: savers born in sixties warned of 2027 apocalypse, 21st March 2012. (http://www.dailymail.co.uk).
[iv] Dan Hyde, Pension age 'could hit 80' for babies born this year, in another budget raid, 23rd March 2012. (http://www.thisismoney.co.uk).
[v] Becky Barrow, Almost half of today's over 50s will be forced to work until 77, warns report, 25 April 2012, (http://www.thisismoney.co.uk).

[vi] Joanne Segars: idem

[vii] Joanne Segars: idem.

[viii] Private rented housing, (http://www.communities.gov.uk).

[ix] Neil Mansell, *Wage salve to financial freedom*, 2011.

[x] Tom de Castella, Eight radical solutions to the housing crisis, 25th October 2011. (http://www.bbc.co.uk).

[xi] A review of the UK rental market 2012, Grainger PLC. (http://www.graingerplc.co.uk)

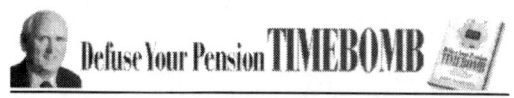
This book is available at

www.defuseyourpensiontimebomb.co.uk

www.amazon.co.uk

www.amazon.com

Also available in Kindle and other e-book formats.

Made in the USA
Charleston, SC
12 October 2012